On the cover- Wise, aged, Chief Spokan Garry
Spokane Indian Tribe of eastern Washington
Sherman Blake, Photographer

July 24, 2022
Annies BookStore
Spokane, WA

*To*
*God be the Glory*

# Chief Spokan Garry

## The First Indian Evangelist West of the Rockies

## Robert D. Bolen, B.A.

3

Spokane anchors, grinders, mortars and splitters
Public Domain

Members of Spokan Garry's Tribe
Public Domain

# CONTENTS

# LIST OF ILLUSTRATIONS

Pend d' Oreille Indian Maiden bedecked in sea shell earrings and
necklace. Her hair has otter fur and weasel skin dangles.
Photo Courtesy of Azusa Publishing Company

## *Acknowledgements*

I would like to thank my wife, Doris Anne for her editing this text and all of the assistance that she gives me. She is excellent at spelling, sentence construction, and a great help to me.

I also want to thank Bonnie Fitzpatrick (the Designer) for her professional formatting and graphic design.

Special thanks go out to the late Teresa Harbaugh, owner of the Azusa Publishing, L.L.C., in Denver, Colorado, www.azusapublishing.com. Over the years, the pictures have really made my books, in my estimation. Teresa had graciously allowed me the use of wonderful iconic American Indian postcard photos in numerous books. Teresa passed unexpectedly last year. She will be greatly missed. May she rest in peace!

A few years back my wife, and son and I had the opportunity to meet and have lunch in Denver with Teresa and her husband. Their website and ad for gorgeous authentic Indian postcards is in the back of the book. I highly recommend that you try their web site. You won't regret it!

Last, but not least, my sincerest thanks to Lightning Source for their fine job of printing this publication.

Spokane Indian Wigwam
Public Domain

# Foreword

An ancient Spokane Shaman named Circling Raven, who was over one hundred years of age related the story from tradition of an old chief and medicine man named Shining Shirt. The legend was told by the Columbia Plateau Flathead and Kalispell Indians.

The prophecy came before his grandfather's birth, who prophesied of a savior. Grandfather had died long before horses arrived. Shining Shirt foretold of the sacred Power that made a great revelation and spoke of good and evil they knew little of and predicted that men would come wearing long black robes to teach the truth. Indians had not heard of white men. Sacred Power gave Shining Shirt a powerful talisman.

The Power told the people, there was a god called Amotkan, "He-who-lives-on-high" and that it is the duty of the people to pray to him. At the turn of the 19th century, Uuree-rachen or Circling Raven, a Spokan Indian shaman, received prophecy about white men arriving who knew the Creator. He had a dream and prophesied the white skinned ones would bring the Leaves of Life, "the Bible." None had ever seen a white man, but fur trappers came bearing Bibles; the Spokan expected them.

A great religious spiritual leader with much wisdom was to come among them. His name was Chief Spokan Garry, who fit the foretold prophecies about religion. Garry came with a Bible, preached of good and evil, and spoke of Jesus Christ. He visited many tribes in the Columbia Plateau preaching the word of God and baptizing the converts. Garry taught of the Lord Jesus Christ and took on the task of evangelizing and baptizing the new converts. The name, Chief Spokan Garry would become well known to the people of the Pacific Northwest, as Garry continued to preach. The chief was known far and wide among the Northwestern tribes. Spokan Garry became the first American Indian evangelist on the Columbia Plateau.

Young Spokan Garry
Fort Colville 1861
Public Domain

# CHAPTER ONE
## THE SALISH PEOPLE

Spokan Indians of the Columbia Plateau spoke the Central Coastal Salish dialect. Three Spokan-Kalispell dialects are Flathead, Kalispell (Pend d' Oreille), and Spokan. Spokan in their tongue means, "Children of the sun," or "Salmon trout people."

The Spokan were semi-nomadic and moved around nine months of the year to hunt and gather, fishing in camps and at Spokane Falls during the salmon runs settling in villages during the winter and shared territory with the Coeur d'Alene, Coleville, and Nez Perce tribes. Polygamy was practiced.

The Spokane tribe of Chief Illim-ee-kum-spokanee included the Lower, Middle, and Upper Spokan bands. He insisted that the Spokan Indians should be called the Spokanee. He was the principal Chief of the Middle Spokane (Spokan) band. In their language they were the Sma-hoo-men-a-ish, Sqeliz, or "the people."The Upper Spokan was the Sin-too-too-ish. The Lower Spokan was the Skai-schil-tinish or People at the Little Falls, who fished for years on the Spokane River. Semi-migratory their territory spanned millions of acres.

The elders spoke of the time when the Salishan (Salish) people were all one, but as their population grew, some Salish split off into different smaller bands: the Coeur d'Alene, Colville, Okanagan, Pend d' Oreille, Salish, and Spokan, to name a few. Salish Indian populations were once estimated at 20,000 strong. After the Smallpox epidemics their numbers were reduced by half.

The Spokane sweat lodge was yet the cure-all for most ailments. The social event was for the men to bathe in the sweat lodge by the Spokane River. Hours of sweating out the impurities, followed by a plunge into the ice-cold river was healthy.

Circling Raven was angry at God. Half their tribe had died of the white man's smallpox. His son, Two Bears had the fever

13

Spokane Indian Fishing
Public Domain

for five days before breaking out with red spots and had finally died. The shaman began tearing down the wooden salmon racks. He yelled, "Here brother dogs, eat our fish," and tossed a fish to the dogs that were barking frantically at his wild antics, "and when the winter comes we will eat you. What difference does it make? or maybe we will eat each other and simply die like dogs." Chief Illim-spokanee emerged from his lodge, as Circling Raven vented his rage. He fell to the ground weeping broken-hearted.

Illim-spokanee consoled his brother; when the sun was overhead he said, "My brother, you must not give up your faith. You have lost your way because of the sickness. It may not be killing your body, but your spirit has the fever." The tribe believed Circling Raven's prayers to the Creator saved them from extermination during the smallpox epidemic of 1792. The Shaman used red ants to devour the pus from the smallpox to heal the sick. He also prophesied the coming of the "Leaves of Life."

Salish tribes dwelled in Montana, across Washington, and British Columbia north of the Columbia to the Pacific. Traditional lands of the Pend d' Oreille and Salish were in western Montana east of the Rockies, north into Canada, west into Idaho, eastern Washington, and south into Wyoming. Spokan Indian territory extended from eastern Washington into Oregon and Idaho. They dwelled near Coeur d'Alene, Kootenai, Nez Perce, Pend d' Oreille and Salish tribes and rode over the Bannock Trail into Montana.

The Cayuse Indian tribe introduced the Spokan Indians to horses around 1730. A famous breed raised was the Cayuse pony. The name, "Cayuse Horse" was used in western slang to mean a Mustang pony. Horses, introduced in the 16th century, provided the biggest source of change in the American Indian culture. The Nez Perce and Palouse (Palus) Indian tribes specialized in Appaloosa horses, bred and raised the spotted horses. Chief Illim-spokanee would grunt and walk away if the barter did not suit him. In 1805,

Salmon Fighting Upstream
Wikipedia.org

six years before Garry's birth, three Spokan braves were down on the Snake River. They encountered the paleface Lewis and Clark expedition party traveling in big canoes. The Spokan traded with the Coastal Salish and the white fur traders for furs.

Spokan Garry was born on a grand day in 1811, the son of Spokan Indian Chief Illim-spokanee, a one-eyed elderly tribal chieftain in the Marian Village at the juncture of the Spokane and Little Spokane Rivers. He was named, Slough-keetcha. Garry was born in a long line of chiefs. His mother had died in childbirth. He had an older brother, Sult-zee and a sister, Qunit-qua-apee. Garry was the youngest and grew up near Spokane River and played with other Spokan children, learned to ride horses as a youth.

As a boy, Garry loved to hear stories of the old days, how Circling Raven prayed and God saved his people and he prophesied about the Leaves of Life, the Holy Bible.

Garry's father related an old tale he had heard from Chief Cornelius. "There was a great thundering in the sky and the ground shook. The next day everything was covered in ashes." Scared and confused, they believed it was the end of the world! They called the volcano fire dragon.

An old man appeared, raised his hand and said, 'Be quiet, I have a message for you.' He said. "This is not the end of the world. More must come to pass before that time arrives. Let me tell you this! People with different colored skin speaking another language and wearing peculiar clothes will come to us before the world ends and will bring teachers who will show us how to learn from marks made on leaves bound together in a bundle. The world will continue until they come. Let us get to work to clean up these ashes." The thunder and ash was the 1790 Mt. St. Helens eruption.

When the white man came, the Spokans called them Boston's and King George's Men. They referred to Canada as "King George's Country." Traveling across America to the Indian

17

Appaloosa Horse
Photo Courtesy of Wikipedia.org

was explained as crossing the backbone of America. Finlay and McDonald, North West Company fur traders arrived just a few months before the birth of Spokane Garry.

After the trappers arrived, Chief Illim-spokanee called a council. Finley and McDonald attended. They decided the Spokan's would allow them to build a post at the confluence of the Little Spokane and Spokane Rivers.

So McDonald built a small post there and trade was established between the local Indians and the white man. They traded beads, blankets, calicoes, guns, knives and woolens to the Spokane for berries, furs, horses and salmon.

Chief Illim-spokanee moved his village across river from the Spokane House. A village was made up of a group of permanent lodges consisting of willows bent in arches, criss-crossed, and covered with bison skins.

He sent Garry on an errand and told him, "Take a canoe to Spokane House and ask Mr. Ross for four new knives. The old ones are wearing out, and women need new ones to clean and cut the fish. Tell him we'll pay him what's fair later." Garry did as he father said. He took a canoe and paddled down-stream to the Spokane House.

When he arrived at the Spokane House, trappers were there at the time. Garry met with Alexander Ross, who said to Garry, "They tell me that Governor George Simpson of the Northern Division will be coming by here next spring-he's a big chief in the company and your pa would want to parley with him. Think you can remember to tell him all that?" "Yes sir," said Garry.

"Good, 'cause your father keeps pestering me 'bout religion, but Governor Simpson is the man who can tell him everything he'll ever want to know about God. Am I right, Jeb?" The trappers listened as Ross went on. "So, you can tell the chief that," Ross concluded. Garry nodded in assent as he departed.

Ancient Spokane Indian Campsite
Public Domain

In the spring the squaws (Spokane women) and their children moved down along the Spokane River below the falls to gather edible roots near Garry's birthplace. Women dug edible roots from the fertile soil that were part of their sustenance. The women dug the bitterroot or clock-qua-loos-sah, in their tongue.

One root that was a major part of their diet was the camas root that the squaws dug with a digging stick or stone tool. The men dug a pit six feet long and lined it with stones, while the boys gathered wood to burn in the fire pit. Grasses and leaves were used to cover the red-hot stones. The camas was carefully laid on the grasses for about 10-12 hours to cook and cool. The camas was then dried in the sun and it was then pounded into flour to make bread or stored in reed containers for winter.

Salmon hatched in fresh water and migrated to the Pacific, fought their way upstream and returned to the stream of their origin to spawn in the autumn.

The females agitated the bottom gravel, wriggling her body to make her nest (a red). Eggs (roe) were then laid. The red contained milt and eggs fertilized by the male before the adults died. A contest was held for the first Salmon harvested and also for the first berries picked.

The Spokane's fisheries were at the juncture of the Columbia and Spokane rivers, where the Spokane and Little Spokane rivers join. In July, the whole tribe fished for salmon. Spokane Falls was a favorite gathering place, fishing spot and trade center. The falls kept the salmon from climbing the river.

Indians used willow basket traps, bows and arrows, harpoons, nets, and poisons to catch salmon and used weirs: piles of rocks built 50 feet apart underwater that slowed the fish. Salmon was smoked over hot coals and was pounded into a pulp to make pemmican or stored. Archeologists have since discovered coastal middens- piles of ancient salmon fish bone, containing artifacts.

Typical Spokane kinship revolved around the nuclear family. This included the mother and father's nearest relatives. The Spokane tribes' religion was a commonality with other tribes of the Plateau. Polygamy was accepted in the tribe.

In the summer months during berry picking time, the people ascended into the mountains to hunt and pick the succulent berries: they picked the service berry, huckleberries, and chokecherries. The next hunt would be the revered buffalo hunt.

In 1824, when Garry was 13 years old, he desired to go on the buffalo hunt with the men. He imagined riding alongside a buffalo and losing his arrows from his bow. Garry knew that if he could kill a buffalo, he would prove himself a man, but Garry's father forbade him to go. Chief Illim-spokanee chose not to hunt the buffalo himself that time and worried about his son's safety riding through Blackfeet country. The Chief was over-protective of his son.  Garry thought, had his father aged that much? Garry wanted so badly to be able to go with the hunting party for buffalo. "But father, you can't say no," groaned Garry as he stood before his father outside their lodge. "I've been counting on this. I'm old enough. I'm ready. I'm a good hunter."

In the lodge, Chief Illim-spokanee sat cross-legged on an old buffalo hide, stoic as a wooden Indian. The skin on his face was aged and sagged.  He was getting on in years and his eyes watered from the campfire smoke. Garry's father said, "You are becoming a good hunter, but I cannot let you go, my son. You are my youngest, my child of promise from the time of the great sickness.  I cannot risk the Blackfeet killing you on the buffalo hunt." The Chief told his brother Circling Raven that he would do well on the hunt with the new rifles bartered from the trading post. Garry  had  ridden his pony up on Lookout Mountain to hunt deer. He was already a good horseman and hunter. He bagged a deer on a regular basis and thought his next plateau was to hunt buffalo.

The Spokanes, led by a hunt chief, rode to the Upper Missouri for the buffalo hunt, knowing they would pass through Blackfeet territory, and could be killed and scalped.

Sometimes the Blackfeet harassed the hunters, like the Comanche did the Ute. This hunt was no different. The buffalo hunters returned with three dead braves draped over their saddles. The Blackfeet had fire sticks (rifles) to defend their territory. Spokane women outnumbered the men, who died in war or on bison hunts; most men had 2 or 3 wives.

Females and children were stolen during raids on the Columbia Plateau. They were kept as slaves or taken for wives. Others were sold or traded. Wealth could be determined by the number of horses or slaves that a man owned. Squaws did the work in the village.

The Spokane buffalo hunters had managed to kill 6 bison, hardly enough to last the winter. The Spokane Indians decided to post a lookout from then on, when traveling through Blackfeet Indian country or they would cross in great numbers, joining other tribes, like the Shoshoni did for protection.

In lean years when buffalo were scarce, the Spokane substituted Hudson Bay's blankets for buffalo robes to keep warm on the cold blustery winter nights. Indians heated stones and inserted them under the blankets for warmth. A warrior might have more than one wife to keep him warm under many buffalo robes. Sadly, many elderly Indians froze to death during the frigid winter blizzards. A central hearth in the teepee added warmth from the cold.

Buffalo was gold to the Indians. Buffalo meat saved them. Spokane Indians made jerky from the buffalo meat. They used the horns for costumes and hoofs for glue. Bones were made into tools and weapons. Gut was used to fastened arrowheads to shafts. The hides less hair was used to construct teepee walls.

Curley Jim
Friend of Garry's
Public Domain

,

# CHAPTER TWO
## FUR TRAPPERS FROM THE NORTH

In 1807, David Thompson trekked the Rockies west to raise fur trade posts for the North West Company and built the Spokane House on the Spokane River on the meeting ground of the Spokane Indians. They called him, Koo-Koo-Sint (the Stargazer). He gave Chief Illim-spokanee a trade-gun. Finan McDonald, a burly 6 foot, 4 inch Scott and other beaver hunters built a cabin or lean-to, the first permanent white settlement in Washington. Finan wed the daughter of a Pend d' Oreille Indian chief, who was Thompson's guide and hunter. Spokane House made profits for two years from furs The Spokane traded for axes, beads, and knives. The Little Spokane River, a slow meandering river, was a source for beaver.

In 1812, John Jacob Astor's Pacific Fur Company arrived in Spokane territory to compete in the fur trade and built a fur trade post near Spokane House on a grand scale, a social place to gather for employees parties. The Spokane were friendly to them and learned some white man's ways, building plank homes in the mountains and also fishing huts. Bill Sublette and Jedediah Strong Smith attended the trade fair at Horse Prairie. Smith was a hunter, trapper, and explorer, who carried a Bible and a long rifle; he was called the "praying trapper." Various tribes came to trade their furs, including four lodges of the Spokane.

Jedediah came back from camp after taking his horse to the grassy area to feed and hobbled his horse. He turned to greet the white haired old Chief Illim-spokanee, with one eye, who was Garry's father. The Spokane Chief started a dialogue using the sign language, a mix of Salish, and some English. "I have learned that the Bostons come to us across the backbone of the world." Jedediah replied, "Yes, we are Bostons, come from the east." "Talk is, Bostons buy furs. Old Pierre say, Bostons pay more." "Pierre is right. Bostons pay more. We Bostons come from over yonder.

Maybe soon, we trade with Spokanes? Pay more money!" "It is good! We welcome Bostons! Come next year you have guns, knives, axes?" "Yes, our chief brings these things even now for trade." "Spokanes like trade. Spokanes trade with Bostons. It is good," Jedediah signed. The elderly Chief developed a fondness for the American. He and Jedediah were all smiles. Jedediah's face showed the hideous scars of a Grizzly bear attack. He was a seasoned mountain man, who had crossed the Rockies. Talk shifted to the "Master of Life." The old Chieftain was keenly interested in Christianity, but had not yet learned the name, "Jesus." The Chief pointed to his Bible. "The chiefs of the white man always carry leaves bound together. Does it teach of the Master of Life? What is this medicine?" "What is the Bible?" Jedediah's heart beat faster; he had dreamed of sharing the gospel with the Indians. He was caught off guard. He showed the Bible to the Chief. "The Bible teaches of God. It says, God sent to earth His son, to show His love for us. The God who made us sent His only son, an express message to every nation."

"Ah! He-Made-Us has a son? Quilent-satmen (the Creator) has a son?" "Yes Quilent-satmen has a son." "Ah!" Illim-spokanee was amazed; it was a new concept for the Chief, who told his people to hear the white man. Believing books were leaves sewn together Chief Illim-spokanee called the Bible, "Leaves of Life." "The Creator had a son!" They had sought the news since Circling Raven's prophecy. The light was dawning. Jedediah's eyes gleamed as he continued. "He has a name too, the son of He-Who-Made-Us, His name is Jesus." "Ah! Jesus!" "Yes, you got it." "What does the name mean? Jesus?" "It means; 'He saves us.' "He-Made-Us sent His son, He saves us. Why such a name as this?" "He-saves us by bringing peace with God and each other and from death. He wants us to live forever with God-with Quilent-satmen." Jedediah was uneducated and unable to explain

26

much more about Jesus and God. The word of God had reached at least one Native American from a fur trader. This was just the beginning of a "Great Awakening" among the Indians of the Columbia Plateau.

In 1821, the Hudson's Bay and North West Companies merged and the Spokane House changed to a Hudson's Bay Trading Post. HBC Governor Simpson visited the post in 1824 and decided to move it, since the swift Spokane River was mostly un-navigable; furs were being depleted.

In the winter of 1824-25, Ft Vancouver was established in Oregon Territory by Dr. John McLaughlin, factor for the HBC. On the 16th of March 1825, the Hudson's Bay employees readied four canoes for the trip to depart from Fort George. Ten company men remained at the fort for a few weeks before abandoning it; Chief Factor John McLaughlin stayed at his home in Jolie Prairie.

The Chinook Indian tribe under Chief Comcomly lined the shore for the send-off, but was sad to lose their fur trade. Cassacas, chief of an enemy tribe, had threatened the party. They embarked in the canoes and paddled on to Jolie Prairie, before going on to Fort Vancouver. In the winter, men from the Spokane House built long boats to go down river in the spring. Simpson advised them to move the post to Colville near Kettle Falls, by the sea. HBC employees made the move in 1826. Jacob Finlay and family stayed at Spokane House; Jacob died in 1828.

Alex Ross, a Scot, received a letter from HBC (Hudson's Bay Company) Governor George Simpson, who said that he planned to come to Spokane House in the spring and had spent the winter at Fort George on the mouth of the Columbia. Simpson told Chief Illim-spokanee he wanted to speak to the important Spokane chiefs in the area and inform them of his visit and impending powwow. Some of the Hudson's Bay employees, namely Dr. John McLaughlin did not like or hire Garry and was biased against

27

educating Indians. Simon McGilllian, who was in charge of Fort Colville a friend of Garry's suggested McLaughlin hire him, but he did not like Garry and flatly refused. He disapproved of Garry's reproach of chief's flogging of tribal members that stole, for instance. The Hudson's Bay Company approved of the practice. Proselytizing Indians to become Christians who helped convert whole villages to become civilized seemed to be a good practice.

Reaching Fort Vancouver, Simpson and crew met around the flagpole. Bagpipes played as Simpson struck the flagpole with a bottle in order to christen the post, in honor of the HBC, naming it "Fort Vancouver" and said "God Save King George, the Fourth." The crowd cheered, "Hip, hip hurray, hip, hip hurray, hip, hip, hurray!" The Governor and his men rode back to Red River. The trip from Fort Vancouver took 18 days. They ate salt pork and beef. The party pulled their canoes up onto the shore at Okanogan. A Kutenai chief waited to counsel with the Governor.

The chief's people had heard Gov. Simpson might arrange for someone to teach them about the Master of Life. News spread about the Master of Life from village to village. Chief Illim-spokanee asked his son Garry to sit near him by the fire in his lodge and asked him if he would go around to the other villages and tell them about George Simpson's coming. Garry was reluctant. The Chief said, "Do you want to go?" Knowing it was a three day trip over snow and ice, Garry replied "Why?" "You could ask a friend to keep you company," Garry was a good horseman, he again spoke, "Any good brave can hunt buffalo," knowing Garry was angry about the hunt.

Garry said, "Send someone else," and walked from the lodge surprised his father had not insisted he go. He saw a brave ride out. Garry noticed a Kutenai chief's son, Pelly, a brave about his age. Garry had not been in favor of being exiled, neither had the Kutenai boy. Garry wondered about Canada, far away.

Spokane River
Photo Courtesy of Wickipedia.com

Garry's Uncle Circling Raven said the Nez Perce saw huge piles of bison carcasses on the plains from the pale-faces' carnage.

After about three weeks and receiving the Chief's message, the other Spokane chiefs began to arrive at the village and also delegations from neighboring tribes. Eight chiefs arrived, wearing fancy headdresses and their finest garb. The festivities began with dancing and feasting. Male garb normally consisted of a deerskin shirt, loincloth, and moccasins. Braves held horse races and Garry often won many of the races. The Chief spoke in sign language.

Garry whispered to his father, "Tell the white chief that I can beat anyone in a race to the top of Pine Bluff, around the lone pine, and back down here to the camp, if he will put up his rifle as the prize" pointing to the old pine tree and then to Governor Simpson's gun to make his point. Simpson was amused, "He wants to race for my rifle?" Ross confirmed the challenge. The Kutenai boy seemed interested. Simpson spoke, "Tell the boy and the chiefs that it is a deal" pointing to Garry and the Kutenai boy.

Chief Illim-spokanee was outraged, "What?" He caught part of Simpson's message. "Do you think we are all dogs that we would give up our children provided they will let me have those two boys to take to Canada," the Chief articulated. Red-faced, the Chief said, "Take them to who knows where?" He stood and wrapped his blanket around him.

"Wait, wait," said Ross in the Spokane tongue. "I'm sure the Governor did not mean any insult. Now chief, you are always asking me about religion, about the Bible, the book you call the Leaves of Life. Well, that's all the Governor is saying. He's offering to take your son-young Garry and that Kutenai boy-to study religion at the best Indian school in Canada."

"Yes," the Governor stood and said, "I want to take a couple of your bright young boys to learn how to know and serve God. Then, after four winters, they can come back here and tell all your people what they've learned." The Chief relaxed. "You would teach my boy about "Quilent-satmen?" "Quilent-satmen?" Simpson frowned at Ross and pointed to the heavens. "God...Quil-something or other, whatever you call Him." "Their word for God, it means Creator of all" Ross said, "Of course! I would take them to Reverend Jones at the missionary school, and there he would learn about God." "You can take a hundred of our children." The Chief spoke to the other chiefs in different dialects, and they all nodded. The Kutenai chief pushed his son forward. Chief Illim-spokanee sat down. Simpson, Ross, and the other chiefs sat down cross-legged around the campfire. The Chief lit his pipe.

"What about my Horse race?" Garry whispered in his father's ear. "I want to win the rifle." "Don't worry about it my son," said the Chief over his shoulder. "You will be the greatest chief our people have ever known-not by winning a horse race or killing buffalo, but by bringing home the Leaves of Life." The Kutenai chief knelt down in front of his son. The brave was shaking his head no and crying his eyes out, not wanting to go.

Garry mounted his Paint and rode across the meadow, up Pine Hill cresting the plateau. His horse slowed to a walk along a game trail through dense underbrush and arrived at the funeral pyre where his mother's body lay. How did she die? Tears filled his eyes not knowing that she had died giving birth to him. His siblings would not tell him. A raven perched on the platform. He hurled a chunk of wood and shouted, the bird flew away reminding him of Uncle Circling Raven. Why was his father exiling him to Red River; had he wanted to know more about the Creator, why didn't he go himself? "Oh God, if you can hear me, if you will listen me, help me be brave about being sent away! And please bring me back home safely." Where was the Red River School? Would I bring back the Leaves of Life? The wind was in his face, as he spurred his pony into a gallop and rode toward his village.

Anglican Red River Mission School Drawing 1820
Public Domain

# CHAPTER THREE
## SCHOOL IN CANADA

In the spring, Governor Simpson chose four men to head down river in two wooden boats that would carry passengers and supplies. The rest of the party rode horse-back down the steep trail to the canoes. They paddled from there and rowed to shore.

The rowboats arrived at the Spokane House. The Hudson's Bay fur brigade met the Governor, who arrived on horseback. In 1825, George Simpson, the Hudson Bay Governor, met with seven local tribal chiefs at Spokane House. He told them he wished to send some Indian boys to the Red River missionary school. Ross, the little Scot, brought a Flathead and a Kutenai chief from the Flathead Post to the lodge of Illim-spokanee. They sat cross-legged on buffalo robes around a horse-dung and pine fueled fire. One-eyed Illim-spokanee passed the pipe to smoke with the chiefs.

Ross used interpreters and waved a letter in the air. "The white chief Simpson has written a letter. In it he says he wishes to take two boys of the chiefs of your tribes to a school in the east, where they may be taught by the white men."

Kutenai Chief Le Grand Queque, a younger man than Illim-spokanee, who wore full red face paint, began to speak:

"For many years we have been told of the coming of the white people. But do the white people look upon us as dogs that they think we should give up our children to go we know not where? Do the Long-hairs think we have no love for our sons that we would give them up for such a journey?"

Chief Le Grand Queque continued, "The Lower Kutenais (Kootenais) never crossed the Great Plains on buffalo hunts as the Upper Kutenais did. They were content to hunt the deer and the Salmon that the Old Man, the Creator, had provided for them on their own lands." The chiefs cried, "oy oy!"

Pend d' Oreille Princess
Photo Courtesy of Wikipedia.org

Again, Alex Ross talked, "But the teacher we have in mind is a minister of religion. He would teach your sons the secrets of our religion that they may return and teach these things to you all. Besides, I go with my wife and children. I will take care of your sons like my own. Surely, if the trail be not too hard for my little ones, it be not too hard for your sons."

After a pause, Chief Illim-spokanee spoke, "The Sin-ho-man-aish want the white man's teaching, as do the Salish brothers of the east and the Sanka of the north. Since the days of our fathers who sleep, it has been prophesied that white teachers would come from the rising sun. I have longed for this day, have dreamed of it, when my son will learn from leaves bound together. These things have been hidden from our eyes, but now we will have our eyes opened. You can lead us by the hand share with us the white man's powers. How will we learn these things unless we take the risk? Does Quilent-satmen not watch over us? Did he not speak of these things long ago, which come to pass now?"

The Chief turned to Ross and said,

"As for me, I give you my son, Slough-keetcha, the joy of my life. He is my youngest. He is in your care. Take him and let him go with you. I have spoken."

After some murmuring Le Grand Queque said to Ross,

"If the Long-hairs are ready to share their teaching of the Master of Life with our people, they might have any number of our sons. It is plain that the Long-hairs possess many valuable secrets, which we all want to hear of and learn. I too, join Child of the Sun and Moon in giving my son, my youngest to you."

Other chiefs offered their sons, too honor them. But Ross interrupted, "I have been authorized to take but two. Let me meet the ladies, and I'll be the judge whether they be fit for the journey or no. If you wish to give your son into my care, bring him to this place just one month from today, an' I'll choose the lad most fit."

The next meeting with the chiefs occurred in front of Ross's tent. The chiefs were adorned in finely decorated buffalo robes, while their sons wore three-point blankets on a spring day. Ross and Simpson told the chiefs to be seated on buffalo hides. Again they passed the pipe around the circle, as was custom.

Then the Kutenai chief, Le Grand Queque, addressed them, "My elder brothers it is said that the Long-hairs wish to take our sons to their teachers, to teach them of the Master of Life. We have brought our sons. The traders have agreed to choose which shall be favored to go with them across the Backbone of the world. Choose now. We have long awaited this day. Our sons have agreed to go with you. We can see plainly: the white man knows many things which we long to hear. There is great medicine in the book of the Long-hairs. We wish to know its mysteries. Choose now from our sons, that they may return to us full of the white man's instructions, to teach us better ways. I am done."

Governor Simpson rose to speak. "We will choose two boys from among you. They will go with us to the teacher at Red River, who will teach them what the Master of Life has told the white men. They will return to you after several years." "It is good!" Illim-spokanee grunted; the other chiefs were in agreement.

After conferring with Ross, Simpson spoke again. "We have chosen the sons of Le Grande Queque and Illim-spokanee." The chiefs were silent. They stared into Ross's and Simpson's eyes, showing no emotion, but clasped hands as a gesture of good faith. No more was said and no words wasted. They made their decision, all things considered. Six chiefs chose to keep their favorite sons at home. Two chose to send their sons with the traders.

On April 12, 1825, at the mouth of the Spokane River, the throng of Indians, horses, dogs and voyagers crowded around those getting ready for the journey. It was stormy that day. The rain stopped about noon, preparation was complete. The two families neared the canoes at water's edge. The two chiefs were there to see their sons off. Many relatives gathered around. Slough-keetcha hugged the members of his family one by one. He was short and stocky for fourteen. He smiled to cover his angst, a brave lad. Uncle Chongulloosoon, was the last to say good-bye. The crowd approached George Simpson, waiting near the canoes.

The Kutenai Chief, Le Grand Queque addressed Simpson. "You see, we have given you our children, not our servants, but our own sons. We have given you our hearts-our children are our hearts-but bring them back again before they become white men. We wish to see them once more Sanka, and after that you can make them white men if you like. But, let them not yet be sick or die, we die. Then they are yours."

Governor Simpson shook hands with the Chief and said, "I will do as you ask." Simpson interpreted for Garry and Pelly. "We are glad you boys are making this journey to the Red River Mission where you will learn about God so that you can bring the message back to your people, are you willing?" Both Garry and Pelly nodded. Garry saw that Pelly appeared to be afraid, but they had no choice. Both of their fathers were sending them to the Red River Mission. "I give you these blankets in solemn pledge to do my best to care for you on this journey." He presented each of the boys with a red Hudson's Bay blanket.

The Indian women began mourning and wailing, which unnerved the Governor. Chief Le Grand Queque told the crowd to be quiet. They surrounded the two boys, and became quiet again, but the dogs had begun to howl.

The Chief spoke, "Do not weaken them with your wailing. They are men, being sent out on a man's quest. Make their hearts brave as you would if they were going on a buffalo hunt." Then he stepped forward and took the boys' hands and placed them in the hands of Alexander Ross. "It is your task, our sons, to bring back to us "the Leaves of Life." Do not fail us! Do not fail the old prophecy." The old Chief walked away and the villagers followed.

Garry, Pelly and the rest of the party mounted their horses and rode along the trail that led to the Spokane River, but he could not look back or say good-bye, knowing he would not see his father for some time. Garry's brother Sulz-lee would accompany them as far as the Columbia, and return to the village with the horses.

Governor Simpson needed to assure the families of the boys' safety on the trip. He reached for the Common Book of Prayer from his pack and opened the book and began to read the baptismal service. He put his hand into the water and baptized the boys choosing the names of two prominent Hudson's Bay traders. He named Slough-keetcha for his tribe and Nicholas Garry. "I christen thee Spokane Garry" sprinkling water on his head and baptized Le Grand's son; "I christen you, Kutenai Pelly," after Robert Pelly. Simpson turned to the families and said, "These two boys are now under the protection of God, whose ways they are going to learn." Simpson baptized the two giving the boys Christian English names to impress the natives by the ritual, the first Indian baptism west of the Rockies.

The Governor performed the baptism, although he was not clergy. The Spokane Indians were used to changing names as their custom. The Christian baptism calmed no fears. The families left not wishing to prolong the heartache of separation. Spokane Garry trusted his father's will, accepting his new name and the rules of the white men and would adhere to them. Garry accepted them as he trusted the Creator. The Chief took each of the boy's hands and put them in Alexander Ross's hand before they left. The party mounted horses and rode to the shore where the canoes were awaiting them.

# CHAPTER FOUR
## THE JOURNEY

The boys were in Ross's and Simpson's care. They climbed into the dugout, departing on the long journey. Garry was fourteen, one of two Indians chosen to be schooled at Fort Garry, Rupert's Land, later named after Nicholas Garry. His father sent him to the Red River missionary school in Winnipeg, Manitoba to be educated at the Anglican mission school. Garry brought an extra pair of moccasins, the beautiful red Hudson's Bay blanket that George Simpson had given him, and his bow and a quiver of arrows. His knife and tomahawk hung from his belt. Pelly was their other choice. He also had his red Hudson's Bay blanket and brought along his bow and quiver of arrows. When they departed, their fathers exclaimed, "Bring them back to us!" Sarah, an Okanogan Indian woman accompanied the group.

Fort Garry was a Hudson's Bay Company trading post that lay on the confluence of the Red and Assiniboine rivers. The post was established in 1822 on the site of Fort Gibraltar where Winnipeg was established for the North West Company. The Fort was named after Nicholas Garry, deputy governor of the Hudson's Bay Company, and then renamed Upper Fort Garry. The members of the expedition party paddled their dugout canoes upstream from the fork of the Spokane River the first day.

They rose very early the following day making better time up river across the mountains. At times they had to abandon their canoes and make portage. The party had to ford the stream dozens of times. They became drenched and cold at every crossing. Wearing only moccasins for footwear was a terrible ordeal for the Indians. They became wet and their feet were numb from the cold and ripped to shreds from the trek. Each man carried an 80 pound knapsack that seemed to weigh a ton. They complained of muscle ache and fatigue. Their feet were bloody and bruised.

They trudged up the mountain pass. The snow at times was two feet deep. At higher elevations the snow and cold were unbearable. At times they walked on ice as the river flowed beneath it. Sometimes ice broke through with every step. Occasionally they had to wade the frozen river hanging on to one another's hands to keep from being swept away by the current.

Garry and Pelly were so numb from the cold that they could hardly stand to walk; ice impregnated their skin in the freezing cold. Fourteen year old Pelly broke down and wept bitter tears, the journey was so hard. His only consolation was the sacred medicine pouch that he wore around his neck and its powers. He was very homesick and suffered from the intense cold. Pelly dreamed of his warm lodge and sweat lodge at home and thought of his family far away. His wailing was so loud that it filed the air. He could not quit crying. As Pelly cried, party members ignored his sobbing.

A phoebe bird sang its cheery song. Spokane Garry told his friend that the bird was singing "Pelly, Pelly" and the boy quit crying. Pelly's trials lessened. Garry stayed close to his special friend to watch over him. This helped to keep his spirits up. Reaching the mountain summit, the men pitched their tents in the snow; they could not sleep because of the cold. That night, Garry and Pelly huddled under several blankets to stay warm and survive.

They trudged through the snow and ice. Spokane Garry and Kutenai Pelly trailed the group. Some suffered from the intense cold and frost-bite. They reached the tree line, where the snow banks reached seven feet in depth and the climb became steeper. The party endured great hardship and sacrifice on the long trek at times nearing mutiny. The snow blew in a fury until the men disappeared from sight. Eyes stung from the driven snow. At night, the trekkers huddled around the campfires getting warm from the bitter cold, but the following morning their clothes were still wet.

Simpson issued a small amount of whiskey for each traveler to try and take the chill off. Isaac, a member of the party had previously gotten drunk, broken a keg of whiskey and threwn his packsack of supplies into the river. Simpson said "That imbecile, as if our rations weren't scarce enough already." As the party trudged over the mountain, they encountered a band of Iroquois Indians, who were obviously drunk. There they stopped for breakfast and later passed by the Iroquois Indians.

It was then that they heard a loud roar sounding like thunder, as an avalanche of snow plunged down an adjoining mountain, but it was a safe distance away; the men realized how lucky they were. Clouds of snow filled the air. The trip over the mountains was unbearably cold. Everyone carried a walking stick. The trek had gone on for weeks. Mid-morning the lead scout saw a band of spotted horses coming toward him and gave a shout!

After traveling for weeks they finally reaching the River mission school, where they were greeted by Reverend John West. He was the first Anglican missionary in the American West. He established the Red River Settlement for Indian boys and looked upon the Indian child as the leader of the wandering race. His objective was to educate the tribes and lead them to Christ.

Governor Simpson wrote to the school petitioning for ultimate care of the two boys lest any tribal warfare result. Spokane Garry met David Douglas, the famous botanist, at Red River and inquired of him about his father and brothers, whom Douglas had met. Douglas said that Garry spoke good English. When Garry and Pelly arrived at the Red River Mission School run by Black Robe David T. Jones, Missionary of the Church Missionary Society of the Anglican Church of England, they were schooled in the Bible and the Book of Common Prayer and were taught agriculture and survival skills. They had to learn European history and geography. The boys had been singled out to be educated. At Red River, Garry learned to speak, read, and write English and French. He learned math and became a Bible-quoting Christian. Garry surrendered his heart to Christ.

His father sent word from home saying, "Your father, Old Chief Illim, asked about you and said he wants you to study hard and hopes you are well. The salmon run was good this year, but they didn't have so many furs to trade." Glad to hear from his father, it caused him to be homesick. Garry and Pelly had worked hard at the school. They remained there for four years until 1829.

On March 25, 1829, George Simpson received word that Garry's father, Chief Illim-spokanee had died. He left Kettle Falls and traveled to the Spokane village before embarking for the Red River Mission. Garry had sent a letter to his father. Simpson journeyed to Red River, where he informed Garry his father died and that the tribes were anxious to see him and Pelly. Simpson stammered, "Er, I regret to be the bearer of bad tidings, but your father passed away this year. Regretfully, you will not see him when you return," but he was unsympathetic to the Indians.

Garry was sad, overwhelmed and close to tears, when Kutenai Pelly entered his room. They shared a time of grief together. He missed his father the most. "We can't assume that our villages will be as we left them," Pelly said, eager to return home.

In the spring of 1829, when Garry was 18 years old, he left school after four years of study, to return to his village. He and Kutenai Pelly began the 1800 mile trek back to Spokane River with the Hudson's Bay trappers. At the mission Garry and Pelly were both given two leather bound books, one was the Common Book of Prayer of the Church of England and the other, a King James Version of the Holy Bible. Now they were going home. Garry looked forward to seeing his people. Garry remembered what Mr. Worthington had said about farming in the absence of game and how he argued the possibility of finding game.

In 1829, the tribes of the Inland Pacific Northwest experienced a vast spiritual awakening spearheaded by a brilliant Native American of the Spokane tribe; he was an amazing man. Jesus said, "Blessed are the peacemakers for they shall see God." Spokane Garry was a rising star among the Spokane a principal chief of the tribe, who became a recognized spiritual leader among the Plateau tribes, a peace chief and a peacemaker. He knew the traditional religion, but had converted to Christianity. Garry had learned English, French, and the Episcopal faith and together with Pelly were the only English speaking Indians in the Northwest. He wore white man's clothes and was a lay preacher to the Spokane and other tribes. He returned home, as the answer to a portion of the prophecy, Garry and Pelly acted as missionaries spreading the gospel of Jesus Christ across the Columbia Plateau.

Garry began his ministry with Kutenai Pelly. In 1829, Chief Spokane Garry and Kutenai Pelly went out to baptize and evangelize the Plateau tribes. They took the villages by storm and performed many baptisms as Anglican missionaries. Garry spoke to the native people in several villages. Garry was the very first Indian evangelist west of the Rocky Mountains who wore white man's attire. Their evangelism spread across the Columbia Plateau preaching to the Coeur d'Alene, Colville, Flathead, Nez Perce, Okanagon, and Pend d' Oreille tribes evangelizing among the Indians teaching them the word of God.

"I am Slough-keetcha the white men call me Spokane Garry. I come from over the backbone of the world, where I ha' been with the white teachers o' the book, at a place called Red River." Chief Spokane Garry observed that the tribe's people did not understanding his English language. He spoke mostly English and had forgotten a lot of his own Salish tongue. Spokane Garry loved the Lord and had led many to Christ at that time. Soon Garry started a school and taught his people.

"Speaking of Garry," Curley Jim a Spokane Indian said, "He told us of a God up above. Showed us a book, the Bible, from which he reads to us. He said, if we were good, that when we died, we would go up above and see God. After Chief Garry started to teach them, the Spokane Indians woke up." (William S. Lewis)

Ellice, a principal Nez Perce chief, who made the trek with Garry back to Red River, had led Lawyer and some Nez Perce to Christ. In 1831, Chief Lawyer led a party to St. Louis for teachers who would return and teach them Christianity.

That year, Garry, Pelly and five more Indians started up the Columbia with the fall brigade of Hudson's Bay employees to return to the mission school and embarked to Lake Winnipeg using small sails on the boats opposed to rowing. The brigade captain chose to row toward Grand Rapids across Moon Lake and started up the Saskatchewan River rowing hard the rest of the way.

The lads had become conditioned working hard with tools at the Red River Mission, rowing from dusk until dawn was not that difficult, but their hands were callused, swollen, and cracked and bleeding. Lastly, they wept. The boys' muscles were sore as they methodically rowed up river. They smeared bear grease on their bodies to fight off the stinging black flies and mosquitoes.

Finally, the party reached Fort Edmonton. At the fort, they rested for four days, long enough to heal their wounds. Garry slung his rifle over his shoulder and mounted his horse and they started off. The fifth day they departed for Fort Assiniboine. Garry and Pelly rode in the direction of Fort Assiniboine, accompanied by members of the Hudson's Bay Company, toward his village on the Spokane River.

Garry's and Pelly's goods were in bedrolls strapped to pack mules led behind their horses. By noon, they had ridden ahead of the party along the trail, their horses began to spook, whinny nervously, side-stepping, and rearing.

Nez Perce Chief Lawyer
Public Domain

### FORT ASSINNIBOINE

The site of Fort Assinniboine is just east of here. This old military post was established May 9, 1879 and built by the 18th U. S. Infantry under the command of Col. Ruger. The troops were to protect settlers from possible Indian raids following Custer's defeat by the Sioux and Cheyenne tribes and the pursuit of the Nez Perce tribe under Chief Joseph. Fort Assinniboine was a base from which the soldiers could sally forth as a reception committee. No serious Indian disturbance occurred, however.

This post was regarded as one of the most strategic points in the Northwest. The Reserve took in the entire Bear Paw Range of Mountains.

General Pershing served here as a lieutenant under General Miles just prior to the Spanish-American War.

In 1911 the War Department abandoned the post. In 1916 the landless Chippewa and Cree found a home on the southern part of the military reserve when 30,900 acres were set aside as Rocky Boy's Reservation and the state of Montana purchased the fort buildings, the land they stood on, and 2,000 acres which became the Northern Agricultural Research Center of Montana State University (Bozeman). Over sixty years of research has improved land productivity through experiments in dry-land farming, crop rotation, summer fallow, shelter-belt planting, strip farming, improved wheat varieties and livestock research.

Sign in Canada to Fort Assiniboine
Photo Courtesy of Wikipedia.org

Then, Garry espied a huge grizzly bear sow with two cubs ahead of them. The cubs grazed off the trail about 25 yards in a huckleberry patch. The sow stood on her hind legs and roared, as her cubs ran off. Pelly tried to keep his horse calm, while Garry rode up behind him and spoke softly, "Just move up slowly. She's not likely to attack the two of us, especially when we are on horseback." Pelly eyeballed the fearsome bear standing in his path.

The grizzly dropped down on all fours, roared, and charged the two boys. The bruin skidded to a stop about ten yards indicating it was a bluff. Pelly's horse panicked and bolted up the trail at a full gallop. Garry attempted to hold his horse steady with all of his strength as it snorted, reared and laid its ears back in fright. The grizzly, moaning, charged after Pelly. The horse wanted to retreat, but Garry kept her on the trail. He let out repeated war-cries to distract the bear as he kept up the pursuit. Garry was an accomplished horseman, but this was different. He had to continue on a shy horse in pursuit of a terribly angry grizzly bear. Garry spurred his mount in an attempt to try to save his friend.

Pelly's terrified horse careened 30 feet down a ravine. His pony slipped and tumbled down the embankment throwing Pelly off as Garry watched in horror. He gave his pony full rein as he drew his rifle from its scabbard. The grizzly did not hesitate as it plunged down the slope. Garry dismounted and took aim with his rifle, just as Pelly's horse ran off. The grizzly headed toward Pelly, who was lying next to a boulder, Garry took aim, but his rifle misfired. He adjusted the flint and fired again; the bear ran off.

Pelly was safe. "Pelly, Pelly are you okay? She didn't get you did she?" Pelly moaned and tried to sit up. With a whimper of pain Pelly grimaced and collapsed against a boulder. He coughed up blood. "Stay still, let me help you," Garry said as he knelt beside his friend, who cried out in agony as Garry tried to move him. They walked unhurriedly to the trail crossing. At times, Pelly coughed up more blood. His shoulder was very painful.

Eventually, the H.B.C. trappers caught up to them. Their horses sauntered down the ravine. "Where are your horses?" one trapper asked. Learning the episode of the grizzly, the man continued, "Figures. My horse has been wanting to jump out from under me. Must'a smelled that old bruin."

He got off his horse and walked over to Pelly. "Here, let me see that arm." He gently touched it as Pelly grimaced in pain. The trapper had Garry stand behind Pelly as he took hold of his arm and wrenched it with a twist. Pelly screamed in agony, letting out a sigh of relief. His shoulder, though still sore was back in place, the pain gone. The trappers retrieved the lads' ponies and soon they were on their way again. Pelly coughed and spit up blood. "That doesn't sound good to me," said the same trapper, who helped him. "You might have broke a rib and punctured your lung." Arriving at Fort Assiniboine Pelly had a high temperature and had become delirious; he could barely ride. "Take him to my house," Captain McKay ordered. "There's a little room in the back he can use."

Captain McKay gave Pelly camphor to help him breathe; the room reeked with the odor. One morning Garry noticed Pelly's breathing was shallow. Garry stayed with Pelly as he slipped in and out of consciousness. He exhaled and the breathing became faint and then the raspy breathing stopped. "Pelly?" Garry inhaled and watched for him to take a breath. In the candle-lit room Garry prayed his friend would live.

"Pelly!" Garry shook him. "Pelly, wake up! You can't do this! Breathe! Breathe!" But Pelly never drew another breath. Pelly was dead. He had died from the very serious accident after the horse fell with him, critically ill he passed on Easter of 1831.

Red River Drainage, Canada
Photo Courtesy of Wickipedia.org

Pelly was buried April 6, 1831. Garry was sent to Kutenai Pelly's tribe, with the unpleasant ask of telling Pelly's father and the tribe of his death; Garry bi-passed the missionary school and trekked to the Kutenai's village.

It was a long tedious walk back to the Spokane tribe, but Garry was strong. It took weeks to travel that far, but Garry paced himself and kept his strength. He dreamed of the Spokane village and home as he trudged onward.

There seems to be more than one account of Pelly's accident and death. One version states when the horse threw him, he was near his home with his father. Another account stated he died at Captain McKay's house at Fort Assiniboine in Canada. A final version was that Pelly died at the Red River Mission in Canada after being thrown by his horse. Apparently, it was known that Pelly was thrown from his horse and died in 1831 and no other information was available in texts. Some authors of various manuscripts fictionalized a story to fill.

# CHAPTER FIVE
## SPIRITUAL AWAKENING

The Spokane had conceived of one God. They were a spiritual people and readily accepted Garry's religion. They called Bibles and Christian books "white man's books." Garry had taught the word of God. After two years of evangelizing the tribes of the Plateau, Garry returned to Red River with five candidates to be educated at the Mission in 1831: Kutenai Collins, Cayuse Halket, Nez Perce Ellis, Nez Perce Pitt and Spokane Berens.

Spokane Garry returned to his village in 1831 and set up residence across the Spokane River from the abandoned Spokane House to become the Head Chief of the Middle and Upper Spokane tribe an important role as a principal chief of his tribe. He articulated English, French, and the Salish tongue fluently and was spokesman for the tribe. Garry served as the Native instructor and taught school introducing farming methods and survival skills to the Spokane Indians. His instruction pushed the Spokane tribe ahead of other tribes in agriculture.

Garry built a crude Tule mat hut with an earthen floor to serve as the school, in order to teach his fellow tribesmen Agriculture, Christianity, and to read and write English, but food gathering interrupted his sessions. In the winter time, Garry had over 100 adult and children pupils and William S. Lewis wrote that Garry was the first "school teacher" in the Spokane country.

He also used the Tule mat hut as a chapel and held church services and spent the winter with his tribe. Garry used a bell to call the people to worship on Sundays and taught them the Bible and about God. Garry conducted a simple service of hymns and prayers each morning and evening.

He used the Common Book of Prayer for grace before meals. They kept the Ten Commandments and used the catechism of the Church of England. Garry taught them the Lord's Prayer and

Drawing of Spokane Indian Dwellings
near the Tshimakain Mission
Public Domain

brotherly love, humility, and peaceful behavior. The service ended in prayer and amen. Hundreds came to Christ in two short years.

They read from the Catechism of the church. Crosses were placed on graves. Garry's preaching drew crowds of Indians from the Coeur d'Alene, Colville, Flathead, Nez Perce, Okanogan, and the Pend d' Oreille tribes to listen to the sermon on Sundays.

*THE ANGLICAN CATECHISM*
*To love your neighbor as yourself*
*To love your father and mother*
*To hurt no one by word or deed*
*To be true & just in all your dealings*
*To bear no malice in your heart*
*To keep your hands from stealing*
*To keep your tongue from evil speaking*
*To not covet another man's goods,*
*but to earn your own living*

Garry did not return to Red River with the brigade in 1832, but continued his evangelism. In 1833, the Hudson's Bay brigade brought five young Indian theology students home, with their Bibles and prayer books, and the five Indian missionaries from Red River began preaching of Jesus Christ and baptizing. Nez Perce Indian students of the Red River Mission School, Ellis and Pitt had great success in spreading the gospel of Jesus Christ to the Nez Perce and surrounding tribes. Spokane Berens was sick a long time and had remained at the school and died July 19, 1834. That same year, a group of inter-mixed Indians of Cayuse, Chinook, and Nez Perce tribes were observed being led in prayer by a chief on his knees who looked up into heaven. They worshipped the Great Spirit of creation, sang songs, more like chant, in the traditional style. An Indian riding by might have dismounted and stood by with his head bowed in reverence during the service.

Captain Bonneville, a famous Army officer was supported financially by John Jacob Astor. Astor's fur trade rivaled the Hudson's Bay Company at the mouth of the Columbia River. He explored the American West during 1832-34 and promised to provide a new insight of the Native Americans. He built relations and intermingled with them learning their ways. Bonneville admired the devotion of the Nez Perce to God, acting more like saints than not. He noticed they had gotten religion and would not work or pitch their tents on Sunday, nor would they fish, trade or do any kind of labor on that day. He noted that they blended the old religion with the new. Captain Bonneville spent the winter of 1834-1835 among the rival Ute-Shoshoni Indians. He referred to the Shoshonis and Eutaw's. The Shoshoni adapted to observing Sundays, holidays, ceremonies, and devotional dances. The Ute Indians had not heard any of this.

In 1835, Samuel Parker was sent out into the mission field among the Nez Perce Indians to survey the situation. He was amazed to see four hundred Indians crowd into a 20 x 100 foot lodge for Sunday meeting.

Missionaries began to arrive on the Columbia Plateau and Circling Raven's prophecy came true. The Whitman's first established Waiilatpu Mission and Henry Spalding built the Lapwai Mission, where Chief Joseph attended. The Eels and Walkers established the Tshimakain Mission at the Spokane village in 1836. Tshimakain was chosen for the mission site by Rev. Elkanah Walker and Rev. Cushing Eells and their wives as the mission to the Spokane Indians. Reverend Samuel Parker from the American Board of Commissioners for Foreign Missions was sent to observe Christian progress in eastern Washington; impressed by their devotion, he filed a good report.

When missionaries investigated thinking the Hudson's Bay Company had proselytized the Spokane, they found their logic was flawed. Instead, it was Native American evangelist, Spokane Garry, who had first reached the Spokane Indians. Chief Spokane Garry and Kutenai Pelly had laid the groundwork for Christianity in the Pacific Northwest. Garry loved God and was a man of peace. In the spring of 1837, Rev. Spalding visited Garry; he showed him his church and school house. The missionary preached to Garry's Spokanes; Garry interpreted for him. Rev. Spalding was quite impressed with what Garry had done among his people. Other missionaries had sung Garry's praises, but Rev. Walker called the Spokanes 'heathens' and detested their polygamy.

Cayuse Halket evangelized his Cayuse tribe and was a great influence on them. Halket's parishioners were quite accepting of Christianity through his efforts. He taught the word of God and baptized them. Halket died in an accident while visiting friendly Indians early in 1837. Kutenai Collins also died unexpectedly after arriving home. In 1839, Nez Perce Pitt passed away. The Cayuse met for church in the chief's 15 x 60 foot lodge. Members of the tribe assembled here for worship. They met twice during a 24 hour period at sunrise. When the lodge was filled, they sat down cross-legged on the ground before rising to their knees for prayer. The chief acted as the minister. Members led the singing of hymns followed by amen. The service was patterned after the evening service at Red River.

The missionaries, Elkanah and Mary Walker, Cushing and Myra Eells were appointed by the American Board of Commissioners for the Foreign Missions in America, supported by the New England Congregationalists, and the Presbyterians. The Missionaries built cabins and dwelled in them at the mission. They established the Tshimakain Mission in 1839. They arrived among the Spokane Indians, after spending the winter of 1838-1839 with Marcus and Narcissa Whitman at Waiilatpu Mission to the Cayuse. Henry H. Spalding established the Lapwai Mission to the Nez

Perce Indians. Catholic and Protestant missionaries came to the village and were not impressed by the natives' primitive ways. They did not agree with Garry's method of evangelism. He disagreed with their religious views and quit the ministry.

Jesuit Priest Peter J. De Smet arrived among the Flathead Indians on the Columbia Plateau. In his lifetime, the revered priest traveled to dozens of Indian tribes of the west converting them to Christianity and salvation greatly influencing the Indians. Wyeth came to the Walla Walla Indians on the Deschutes River. He described their chief at dawn on Sunday calling the Indians to prayer, followed by a song or chant. They said grace at meals and prayers to the "Great Spirit" in the evening.

Indians seem to retain some of the old traditions. Traces of Catholicism remained among the Nez Perce; they continued to observe holidays of the Roman Catholic Church. Due to the coming of the Jesuit Priests, Coeur d'Alene and Kutenai tribes became Catholic, since Coeur d'Alene and Kutenai students had died at Red River. After all of the conversions to Christianity and baptisms, the Medicine man still played a big role in the Spokane tribe. Scores of Indians had not accepted the word of God.

Garry, Reverends Eels, and Walker Christianized many Spokane Indians and baptized Protestants. Spokane's neighbors, the Coeur d'Alene, became Catholic from the Jesuits' teaching in their village. As they met the Spokane's, they denounced their faith as worthless, taunting them. Garry said that "the evils arising from this state of feeling with a forbearance and Christian spirit of toleration, which would have honored anyone," to George Gibbs, who had accompanied government railroad surveyors in 1853.

The pupils trained in Canada had been nominated by the Hudson's Bay Company, who transported them to Canada. All of this was done in an effort to civilize the Indians. What they learned at Red River became their life-work. The boys were chosen so that they could return to their tribe and teach them Christianity with civility. The Indians became saints instead of savages. The young men prayed for blessings on the tribes; prayers were said and hymns were sung. Christianity had caught on like wildfire!

God revealed Jesus to the Northwestern tribes and the "Spiritual Awakening" began. Surrounding tribes: the Flathead, Kalispell, and Nez Perce began to hear the word of God. All of the Indian prophets agreed that Jesus was the person that they had seen in their visions. The Flathead and Kalispell warriors wore wooden crosses on the battlefield to protect them from harm. The Coeur d'Alene Indian tribe worshipped Jesus Christ at Christmas.

As the missionaries came to their village, they created a firestorm of controversy for Garry and his form of evangelism. Instead of building on Garry's foundation of Christianity, they attacked him. The Indians came under scrutiny from the Catholic Church and the Coeur d'Alene; missionaries were aghast to see Spokane's carousing, drinking, gambling, and smoking.

Garry, embarrassed over his bigamy, avoided the missionaries, unable to compete. Garry quit his preaching at the peak of his influence, but his acclaim faded when the missionaries came. Garry removed his white man's clothing and put on his Indian garb instead, much to the disdain of his critics.

In 1841, Governor Simpson passed through Spokane country and became irate when he saw Indians gamble. He saw his old friend Garry playing cards in an Indian camp on the banks of the Pend d' Oreille River, near Newport, Washington. They were using cards obtained from fur trappers in Spokane country. Simpson referred to the gamblers as hungry, naked savages turning greasy, blackened cards, and said he knew the master of the game.

After the white man missionaries pushed Garry out of the church, he suffered a big blow to his beliefs and he began to gamble and drink with the other Indians.

Joseph, the famous Chief of the Nez Perces, one of the greatest Indians that ever lived. 1903. Before the Chief would pose for this picture and the next he exacted $10 from the artist.

Nez Perce Chief Joseph, Horse-mounted
Photo Courtesy of Wikipedia.org

Garry's decline actually was the coming of the white man. He reacted to the pressures of the missionaries that caused his downfall. The government took their ancestral lands. On the Wilkes' expedition, members of Lieutenant Johnson's crew referred indirectly to an Indian chief, who told them he had once been a great authority over his tribe, but because of his gambling, had lost all of his influence. Garry continued to drink and gamble from 1837-1842.

When Garry was around 30 years of age, he had all but abandoned his duties as chief of the Spokane and his efforts to help the Indians. He had backslidden into gambling and the bottle. Garry also indulged in drinking the "Boston man's fire water."

Spokane Garry drank occasionally, and sometimes got drunk and spent the night in the hoosegow. Garry spoke of it the next day that he really had no business getting drunk the night before. Garry's conduct however was caused mainly by his rejection by the missionaries' criticism of his efforts to evangelize and educate the tribe. Garry quit drinking a few years later.

Chief Spokane Garry became involved as a liaison to the Army. He and 200 Spokanes met October 24, 1853 with Stevens and McClellan at the old Tshimakain mission around the white man's campfire and had an enjoyable time. Garry and Stevens spoke. Garry mentioned a letter he had sent. Stevens had a good opinion of him. Garry invited Stevens and McClellan arrived at his lodge the next day and Stevens found it comfortable.

The Spokane people had become split over Catholic-Protestant differences, but the bias of the missionaries had faded by 1848. Between 1863 and 1866, Catholic Fathers Carvana, Cataldo, Giorda, and Tosi invaded Chief Spokan Garry's Middle Spokane band and held services there. On December 8, 1866, the Jesuits again held services, but in the Upper Spokane Territory. These two bands were Chief Spokan Garry's people.

When Jesuit Father Cataldo came to Spokane territory to establish a chapel, Spokane Garry was absent. Members of his band were rather sheepish about giving the priest license to build a chapel there. Father Cataldo stated that if the Indians did not want the chapel there after three months, he would destroy it. Because of his efforts, almost half of the Spokane there became Catholics.

Chief Spokane Garry came back and was upset. He wanted the Chapel moved or destroyed, but the Catholic converts did not want the Jesuits to leave. They said if he did not like it he could leave. Garry and other Presbyterians in the vicinity hated to see so many of his tribes people converting to Catholicism.

Garry was very well known in the Columbia Basin and in 1871 held a camp meeting for two weeks for a revival. At the same time, Jesuits held a mission for two weeks with a number of the Upper Spokane converting to the Catholic faith. The delegation of Protestants under Spokan Garry sent to Rev. H.H. Spaulding at Kamiah, Idaho (Kamiah is Nez Perce for many rope litters) asking him to visit them and hold revival services. Rev. Spaulding traveled to the Spokane Valley to hold services. Over 250 souls converted to Christianity. Many were baptized by Father Cataldo.

Garry was a Christian convert who would never lose his faith. His contribution to the conversion of the Spokane and other Indian peoples was immense. Whenever a Spokane powwow or religious meeting was held, people flocked to hear Garry.

Garry was born a Spokane Indian along the Spokane River. He was educated in Manitoba, Canada and returned to his people with his new found religion. He not only was accepted by his people, but was revered by the surrounding tribes of the Columbia Plateau. Chief Spokan Garry became renowned in the Pacific Northwest. Because he was an American Indian the missionaries did not accept his methods, although he had brought hundreds of converted to Christ.

Chief Spokan Garry
Public Domain

Jesuit Father Cataldo
Public Domain

# CHAPTER SIX
## WEALTH IN BRIDE PRICE

Indians dwelling east of the Mississippi River were forced to move west of the Mississippi and lodge in Indian Territory in Oklahoma per the Indian Removal Act passed by Congress on May 26, 1830 in order to give the land to white immigrants.

Garry took a Spokane woman for a bride and gave her the name, Lucy. They had a baby girl, Nellie. They were married, but did not get along. She moved out and took their daughter and set up her teepee near the old Spokane House along the river.

Garry engaged in the buffalo hunt. The Spokane joined with other Salish tribes to insure security in Blackfeet country; they formed hunting parties of the Coeur d'Alene, Colville, Flathead, Okanogan, and Spokane Indians. He began with the Spokane and the Colville and rode through Coeur d'Alene country to gain recruits. They continued through Idaho Territory and picked up the Kutenai hunters, then into western Montana, where they joined the Flatheads. From there they rode eastward to the Upper Missouri.

Chief Spokane Garry's years at the Red River mission clearly had set him apart from the other Spokanes. He wore white man's clothes and was an educated man. He walked with pride over his accomplishments and was highly respected in the tribe. Garry preferred a blanket to an overcoat in cold weather and wore just a loin cloth and war shirt, wrapping a blanket around himself. This is what the white man called a "blanket Indian." William S. Lewis, a biographer, described his dress with disdain. Garry was mocked by his family, who lived in considerable comfort having commodities of coffee, flour, sugar and tea.

Nuptials in the tribes were arranged marriages. Garry was 30 and married a 15 year old Umatilla chief's niece in 1841, he named Nina. Garry owned only one horse, his Bible and teepee,

Spokane Falls Drawing
Public Domain

but her parents consented. He received a sizeable dowry of a string of Appaloosa horses. She was his second wife. He bred and raised them. Garry chose white horses for his personal use, possibly riding War Bonnet horses (white horses with dark ears) that became his trademark. Nina and Garry had a daughter and moved onto a farm in an area known as Pleasant Prairie, east of present day Hillyard in Spokane among the Upper Spokane Indians and prospered. He and Nina were very happy together.

In 1844, Garry, Nina and members of the Cayuse, Nez Perce and Walla Walla tribes embarked on a trading mission to California in numbers as security traveling through hostile Indian country. Some considered themselves Christians, but only Garry and Elijah Hedding, son of Walla Walla Chief Peo-peo-mox-mox or Peu-peu-mox-mox (Yellow Bird), were church members. In autumn, the party was fully equipped with horses for travel and enough furs for trade in exchange for cattle. The band continued along the John Day River and then turned south through the rugged and unforgiving lands of the Klamath and Shasta Indians finally reaching Fort Sutter.

They set up camp at Fort Sutter and began their trading. Some in the party were new to California and found new species of trees and fruits. Nina was fond of grapes. The men had success trading for cattle, but lacked enough trade goods to purchase all that they wished before ascending into the mountains, where they encountered hostile Indians.

They fought and defeated them capturing 22 horses and mules and took them back to the fort. Settlers claimed the animals were theirs and demanded their return. The band refused to comply. A conflict ensued; a convict named Grove Cook, who hated Indians, killed Elijah Hedding. The killer immediately fled out the door. Garry narrowly escaped their bullets. The party fled abandoning their horses. When they reached Walla Walla, they

Chief Spokan Garry of the Middle and Upper Spokane Tribe
Public Domain

were angry at the Californians and contemplated going to war, but cooled off and dropped the war idea. They tried to obtain justice through Agent White, but Dr. White left the region abruptly.

Chief Spokane Garry informed Elijah's father, Chief Peo-peo-mox-mox, of his son's death. Peo-peo-mox-mox owned a huge herd of over 1,000 horses. Stevens was invited to visit him and see his herd in order to realize the importance of the Chief.

Ellis, a Nez Perce Indian sub-chief, who was educated at Red River Mission, was to confront Dr. Elijah White to bring the young man's murderer to justice. California law differed from Oregon and Dr. White had no authority. Young Ellis returned to the Columbia Basin, scorned by the other Indians for accepting Dr. White's explanation. The young Chief Ellis lost face with his people.

Major John Owen, an American who owned a trading post at St. Mary's Mission on the Bitterroot in Montana Territory, drove a large string of several hundred horses to winter in Spokane country, for fear of Blackfeet. John Owen and Chief Garry became fast friends. They both raised and bet on races.

In 1846, the Canada-America boundary dispute was settled by the 49th Parallel. In 1851, Washington became a territory. Garry was a wealthy man with a large herd of horses and a big tract of land. His influence among Indian tribes had grown. Hundreds of Indians had gathered to hear Garry preach. He had gained the respect of the tribes people of the Columbia Plateau.

Gold was found near Ft. Colville 1852; miners built cabins on the Spokanes' favorite lands. They overran the hills by the thousands. The trespassers confiscated the Indians' lands with no conscience of their actions. Their cattle ate grasses meant for the Indians' cattle. Miners gave the Indians fire water, slept with Indian women, and stole their horses. Spokane hostilities rose and they were ready to rise up against them and go on the war trail.

Indian Puppy
Public Domain

Walla Walla Chief Peo-peo-mox-mox
Public Domain

Cayuse Indian Warrior
Public Domain

# CHAPTER SEVEN
## ON THE WARPATH

Walla-Walla, Washington is approximately 180 miles from Spokane, Washington, named after the Spokane tribe. In 1836, Reverend Marcus Whitman and his wife, Narcissa founded the Whitman Mission (Waiilatpu), "Place of the Rye Grass," seven miles west of present day Walla-Walla, Washington. Marcus Whitman and the Indians had their problems early. The wild Cayuse Indians clashed with Whitman usually over money or whiskey. The men helped plant the crops and build structures and fences around the fields. The missionaries were provided with horsemeat from the Indians until the crops were harvested.

The Cayuse Indians initially accepted the Whitman missionaries with open arms. Whitman chose Cayuse land on which to build with fertile ground in a forested region. The Cayuse and Nez Perce tribes were friendly. The Mission grew to include a large adobe house, residences, a grist mill and a blacksmith shop.

In 1836, Henry Spalding established the Lapwai Mission at the mouth of the Clearwater River among the Nez Perce Indians in Oregon Territory to convert the Indians to Christianity. Spalding's mission, the first Nez Perce settlement, was 12 miles north of Lewiston, Idaho Territory along the river. He imported a printing press to print the New Testament into the Nez Perce language.

Observing the Cayuse tradition, Indian women did all of the work, Narcissa Whitman tried to change the custom and lit into the tribal chief, embarrassing him. Chief Tilaukait vowed to do some work, but he had a hot temper; he was chief of the tribe they were there to save. In 1837, the Whitman's had a baby girl named Alice Clarissa, who was born on Cayuse land; the Indians called her Cayuse-te-mi (Cayuse girl). Narcissa refused a gift of a pair of coyote paws from Cayuse Chief Tilaukait, which angered him. The tribe was delighted when Alice was born, but she drowned in 1839.

In October, Whitman started back East to try to keep the missions open, crossing the Blue Mountains reaching Fort Hall, Idaho backtracking from Fort Benton, Montana and Santa Fe, New Mexico. In 1843, he joined a trading company, en route to St. Louis. He arrived to seek monies to build the mission, but was advised to abandon the idea. Whitman sold his New York home to raise money and left New York on horseback with pack animals. Reaching the Platte River in Nebraska Territory Whitman then joined emigrants bound for Fort Walla-Walla and headed up the "the Great Migration" of Conestoga wagons opening the Oregon Trail. He wrote to James Porter, Secretary of War, saying he had piloted one thousand settlers with 120 wagons, 700 oxen and 800 cattle to Oregon in 1843 and stopped at Fort Boise where he purchased coffee and flour from the Hudson Bay's Company.

Whitman had promised the Cayuse Indians monies for their land in 1836 that was never paid and hostilities arose. In 1843, in his absence, when Doctor Whitman did not keep his promise to pay them, the Cayuse warriors vandalized the mission during his absence and burned down a grist mill and outbuildings. The Nez Perce tribe demonstrated at Lapwai, but during the massacre, Nez Perce Indians harbored Dr. and Mrs. Spalding, to save them.

Mrs. Whitman fled to Fort Walla-Walla and was later escorted home by the Hudson's Bay Company employees after Rev Whitman arrived in the autumn of 1843. Whitman returned from back east, and did not pay them the money owed. Whitman was living a lie.

Settlers in wagon trains continued to stop at the stage stop and way station alarming the Indians. Hundreds of pioneers stopped along the Oregon Trail. Then, a new blight added to their problems. Unfortunately, the wagons carried measles. People at the mission began to come down with the illness and the Indians began dying and dropping like flies.

Cayuse Indians lost half of their tribe to measles from contact with the Whitman mission. Indians bathed in cold water to reduce the fever, their custom. Whitman warned them, but they bathed in cold water regardless to combat high fever dying as a result. The medicine man called Whitman a devil, blaming the deaths on him, cast a spell and demanded they go on the warpath!

The Whitmans attended the sick November 29, 1847. Mary Ann Bridger was in the kitchen setting the table, when the Cayuse Indians burst in. Cayuse Chief Tilaukait and Tomahas entered demanding medicine. Tilaukait accosted Marcus Whitman and cried out that his third son had died of measles. Tomahas pulled his tomahawk from under his blanket and bludgeoned the Doctor with a blow to the skull, killing him. Mary Ann screamed and ran around the house to the other door. She shouted, "They are killing father." Women and children ran upstairs; the Indians ordered them to come down. The Whitmans and 9 others were murdered; two lay dying. Frenzied Cayuse killed 14 settlers and torched buildings. Women and children were captured; 13 escaped to Lapwai mission; others made it to Fort Vancouver.

During the massacre, the Henry Spaldings were protected by the Nez Perce. One man escaped, but drowned en route to Fort Walla-Walla. Mary Ann Bridger was captured and taken with hostages to Willamette Valley and died a year later of exposure. The Cayuse held the prisoners slaves. A month later, on December 29, 1847, Peter Skene Ogden, of the Hudson's Bay Company, bartered goods to the Cayuse Indians in exchange for the captives. Forty nine prisoners survived and were released. The Hudson's Bay Company brokered 62 blankets, 63 cotton shirts, 12 Hudson Bay rifles, 600 loads of ammo, 7 pounds of tobacco and 12 flints for the captives return. The men of the Hudson's Bay Company were the heroes who saved so many lives that day. The Indian ties were stressed after the 1847 hanging of six Cayuse Indians.

The Army had built a military road from Fort Benton to Fort Walla Walla across Spokane lands. At the time, Isaac Stevens was a young surveyor.

In 1853, Lt. Rufus Saxton advanced from Walla Walla. Chief Spokane Garry recommended they greet the Army in friendship, which they did, but with a show of strength. Garry and 30 Spokane warriors rode to the crest of a hill overlooking the camp and chanted a song of welcome.

The American Army consisting of three officers, enlisted men, 2 civilians, 3 herders, 2 cooks, and Antoine Plante as guide bivouacked on August 6, 1853 in Spokane country. The Spokane warriors stood out in the sunlight, which was impressive.

Chief Spokane Garry rode out in civilian garb, save an eagle feather headdress and deerskin moccasins, to meet the lieutenant. They greeted each other. Lieutenant Saxton was glad to meet an educated Indian.

He explained to Chief Spokane Garry that he was on route to meet Isaac I. Stevens, the newly appointed Governor of Washington Territory, which then included the present state of Washington, the northern half of Oregon Territory, northern Idaho, and western Montana. Stevens was also the Superintendent of Indian Affairs for the new territory.

In a peaceable manner, Garry rode back to his band and they rode into the Army camp. Saxton thought them to be a proud people. They intermingled in friendship. The warriors performed a war dance, for their benefit. The lieutenant gave out a few gifts to Garry and some Spokane and told them they were from the "Great White Father" in Washington. Only Garry understood the meaning.

On October 16, 1853, As Garry rested in front of his lodge, a party of Upper Spokanes, friends whom Nina ran horses with, rode in. The party had important news. The previous evening, they were at Wolf's Lodge, northwest of Lake Coeur d'Alene and encountered a party of white men. A religious ceremony was in progress, when they arrived. After the service they learned that the new territorial Governor was there. He mentioned buying a string of horses. Garry's name surfaced.

Stevens and his party rode to the Spokane House, but Garry was absent and had broken camp to observe the white men. Governor Stevens sent word for Chief Spokane Garry to visit him at his camp, some eight and a half miles west of Spokane House.

Stevens strolled along the river and observed some Spokane Christians during their evening worship. He noted in his diary that the order of their service was the address, the Lord's Prayer, the Psalms and the benediction.

On October 17, 1853, Chief Garry was summoned to meet with the newly appointed Governor of Washington Territory, Isaac Stevens. Stevens was on his way east to the new capital in Olympia, when he stopped by and visited Garry. They talked into the night, speaking both English and French. Garry surprised Stevens with how versatile he was in both languages.

Stevens wanted the Spokane to change their ways. Garry could see the good in adopting the paleface's ways. Not knowing Steven's intentions regarding the Indians, Garry held back on the issues. Stevens was annoyed by Garry's demeanor and wrote in his diary, "Beneath a quiet exterior he shows himself to be a man of judgment, forecast, and great reliability, and I could see in my interviews with his band the ascendancy he possesses over them."

A member of the party spoke of Garry: "he is what he claims to be and what few are among these tribes, a chief." Garry was the principal chief of the Middle and Upper Spokanes. In 1853, there were 500-600 members in the Spokane tribe, who were happy and prosperous.

On October 29, 1853, Garry led Stevens and a party of white men to Fort Walla Walla, Territory of Washington. Garry was riding his favorite white horse. They camped near an Indian graveyard. Garry explained how the Indians used to slay the horses of a fallen warrior and bury them at the same time to provide horses in the hereafter.

On route, they passed a point on Lake Pend d' Oreille, where a mysterious painted rock stood high over the water. The petro-glyph contained images of beasts and men. The Indians believed a race of men that preceded them had made the paintings. The superstitious natives feared if they passed the rock the "Great Spirit" would create a disturbance in the water and drown them. Garry dismissed this as superstition.

The party reached the Snake River on the afternoon of November 1st. They reached the village of Walla Walla Chief Peo-peo-mox-mox on November 5th. Stevens was awed at the sight of the Chief's massive herd of over 2,000 horses. He was a very prosperous chief. They all had a good visit and left on November 8th via The Dalles in Oregon. They traveled by canoe to Fort Vancouver on November 17, 1853 then Garry departed for home.

Chief Garry had made special trips to Fort Colville, Washington to have grain ground into flour in the grist mills there. He conceived of a grist mill to be built on the Little Spokane River, joined by a stream. He made an agreement with a B.F. Yantis, who bought a mill in Olympia and freighted it to the site. It began operation in 1854, but Garry and B.F. Yantis quarreled over the mill. It was soon relocated to Fort Colville.

B.F. Yantis later claimed that Chief Spokan Garry had repudiated the contract, but Chief Garry insisted he had attempted to claim the land under the Donation Act of 1850. The Spokane Indians assisted in tearing down the mill to prevent this. Chief Spokan Garry had wanted the miller to exist on income from their tolls for milling, but he did not desire to have white men on their land.

# CHAPTER EIGHT
## GARRY, THE PEACEMAKER

Garry, Nina and a number of Spokane chiefs and sub-chiefs formed a party in 1854 and left on a mission to the Grande Rhonde Valley in northwestern Oregon to visit the Yakima Indians. Yakima Chief Kamiakin had called a council of many territorial tribes. Governor Stevens had circulated among the tribes saying he planned to make treaties with them. At the council, Yakima Chief Kamiakin warned the tribes of the danger of their numbers and making treaties with the palefaces. He pointed out the dreaded diseases on the Columbia Plateau the settlers had brought with them. He told how under the Donation Act, the white man was encroaching on Indians lands taking the best land as they wished.

Chief Kamiakin favored the tribes going on the warpath with the white eyes and confining them to the coast to keep them from coming overland. Kamiakin heard from Puget Sound allies that Stevens planned to drive Hudson's Bay traders out to prevent Indians from getting more weapons from them. The chief wanted the tribes to go on the war trail to stop the palefaces. Chiefs Garry, Lawyer, and Sticcas were opposed to war. Some of the younger chiefs sided with Kamiakin and were intent on war.

In 1855, Garry was visited by Gov. Steven's Secretary, James Doty, and an Indian agent. He was told that as acting Superintendent of Indian Affairs in Washington Territory, Stevens was calling a meeting of the Cayuse, Nez Perce, Walla Walla, and Yakima tribes to be held in the Walla Walla Valley in May and that Garry and other Spokane chiefs were invited to attend as guests. Garry accepted and was present for the council on May 29, 1855, with nearly 5,000 Indians present. Garry acted as an observer. In a poor showing, only Governor Stevens with 47 dragoons were present as escort. Stevens told them to move onto reservations. He proposed the Cayuse, Spokane, Umatilla, and

General Isaac Stevens
Photo Courtesy of Wikipedia.org

Yakima Chief Kamiakin

Public Domain

**Cataldo Mission**
The oldest Church in Idaho, 1853
Built by the Coeur d'Alene Indian Tribe
Author Photo

Walla Walla tribes go onto the Nez Perce Reservation and the Klickitat go onto the Yakima reserve. Garry had participated in many peace councils.

Stevens spoke with Garry of a third reservation for the Spokane. Indians were promised annuities payable for a 20 year period in blankets, clothing, and other useful articles distributed to tribal members and promised monies to be spent on the reservation blacksmith shops, carpenters, grist mills, mechanics and schools. Changing from living free to life on the reservation, Indians still fished, gathered roots and berries, as well as pastured stock on vacant land. Chiefs Lawyer and Sticcas left happy, as some did not want to let go of their ancestral lands. Peo-peo-mox-mox and Looking Glass would not make their marks but eventually signed.

In 1855, miners and settlers trespassed on Cayuse, Spokane, Umatilla, Walla Walla and Yakima Indian lands creating conflict. Garry knew the might of the U.S. Army and the will of the white-man that poured onto Indian lands in Washington Territory to lay claim to their ancestral lands. In Washington Territory, though the Yakima had signed a treaty, Chief Kamiakin decided to keep the palefaces out of their country and asked other tribes to join them on the war trail. Even after Kamiakin and the Yakima signed the Walla Walla peace treaty, they were ready for the war path. Yakima vowed they would fight the white eyes on Yakima land. The Spokane tribe however wanted no part of it.

In May of 1855, Governor Steven's treaty team arrived in the territory. Stevens was alarmed over the Indian-white man conflict and left on a treaty tour to encourage the tribes to move onto reservations. Palefaces on their lands alarmed them. Stevens called a council at Plante's cabin on the Spokane River, promised friendship and gave the Spokane Indians the choice of selling their lands. Plante, a half-breed, dwelt among the Spokane just below Spokane Falls, farming and ran a ferry across the Spokane River.

Garry pleaded peace with the white man, until they could speak with Governor Stevens, keeping the Spokanes out of war. Miners had been killed on the Yakima River and Yakima Agent Bolton was killed, too. Garry was informed Stevens was coming back from a parley with the Blackfeet tribe and would be calling a council of the Coeur d' Alenes and Spokanes. After council with the Walla Wallas, Stevens knew they would oppose the peace treaty. Garry dreaded war. The situation rapidly deteriorated during the following years. War was on the horizon.

On June of 1855 at the Treaty of Yakima, Cayuse, Umatilla, Walla Walla, and Yakima Indians were forced to cede an excess of 6,000,000 acres to the United States government in part as punishment for the Cayuse Massacre of Methodist missionaries, Marcus and Narcissa Whitman and others at the mission on November 29, 1847.

The treaty was signed on traditional meeting grounds at Walla Walla. The tribes were paid $200,000 for their lands over a prescribed number of years. Chief Kamiakin held off signing the treaty until the last. At the time the treaty was signed, Governor Stevens assured the Indians of the Columbia Plateau that no miners or settlers would trespass on their lands prior to the treaty being ratified, but a gold strike near Colville gave way to miners' encroachment. Passing miners stole the Indians' horses and molested their women.

On October 1855, Yakima Chief Kamiakin and 300 warriors attacked U.S. Army Major Granville O. Haller in the command of 84 soldiers. Instantly, bullets began flying everywhere. The Yakimas had assembled on one side of Toppenish Creek at the ford and Haller's troops were on the other side. The two forces ended in a standoff.

Governor Stevens heard about the Yakima outbreak of war coming back from Blackfeet country, rode up to the Spokane village, and demanded whether they were for war or peace the evening of November 27. He had already mustered troops for war.

There was conflict on the borders of Spokane lands, Yakima Indians to the west and Nez Perce country on the south, but Spokane Garry still kept his young braves in check. Garry wrote to Stevens concerning the pressure he was under.

Garry received a letter, the summer of 1856, from Stevens calling him back to Fort Walla Walla for a treaty with the Nez Perce, Walla Walla, and Yakima. He replied September 12, 1856.

"Sir: You had desired our going to meet you at the treaty, but we cannot go on account of the salmon, which is coming up now, and we are laying in our winter's supply; as it is our only resource for living, we think we cannot do without it. As for us, we are at peace, and it does not make any difference about our not going to meet you, for we all want to remain quiet and peaceful. The Coeur d' Alenes have all left, but one chief, for the buffalo country, and my people are going also as soon as salmon is over. I have heard that the Nez Perce Indians were talking of war."

Garry wrote,

"That makes me uneasy and study much; for my part I don't like to see them take up their arms, for they will gain nothing by it. I have heard that you talk hard about us, by Indians, but I don't believe it; but I think it is all the Yakima's doing, to get us to join them; but I don't believe it, for they want me to go to war by all means; but I would rather be quiet. But I expect you have more confidence in me than that, and I hope you will not believe any of their stories, for I know that you know too much to give credit to such idle talk. When we meet next we can have a good understanding together, for I will keep nothing from you and expect the same from you."

So I remain, very respectfully yours,

"Garry"

Coeur d'Alene Indians
Photo Courtesy of Wikipedia.org

Garry had foreseen the council to be a failure. The party was lucky to get out alive. The Indians had attacked them, but they had joined forces with the troops at Fort Walla Walla and the combined forces had retreated to Fort Dalles to the west.

General John Ellis Wool, Commander of the troops in Oregon and Washington ordered the region closed to white settlers due to the massacre of both friendly and hostile Indians. This created fervor among the settlers, who were anxious to get Indians' lands under the Donation Act of 1850. Congress had failed to ratify Stevens' Treaty of 1855 with the tribes, which only confused them more.

That Sunday morning, Garry and his band met for church and held a simple service in their village. That very morning, Stevens swore 14 miners under Judge Yantis and named them, the "Spokane Invincible." At 2:00 pm, Stevens called Spokane Garry and Coeur d'Alene Chief Vincent and some other chiefs into his tent. Stevens promised to help and protect them and to keep them comfortable. Garry was more interested in hearing about land.

Gary spoke,

"When we talk to an Indian about land, we talk about what it is. When we wish to purchase his land, it is for him to say whether he will sell or not, if he does not wish to sell it he will say so. We shall never drive him from his lands. I want you to think of this. I want you to show me your hearts."

Garry and the other chiefs wanted to change the attitude of their people and the problem of signing a treaty and selling their lands. Realizing the Indians had hostilities against the whites, Stevens enlisted four additional miners to the Spokane Invincibles and formed "Stevens Guards" of 26 miners. Stevens spoke.

"I think it best for you to sell a portion of your lands, and live on Reservations, as the Nez Perces and Yakimas agreed to do. I would advise you as a friend to do that...If you think my advice

85

good, and we should agree; it is well. If you say, 'We do not wish to sell,' it is also good, because it is for you to say"...

Stevens knew that the Indians did not want to sell their lands so he continued to stall by giving them a speech.

Stevens continued, stalling, knowing the Indians weren't friendly with the idea.

"I want every man here to believe that I am and will be his friend, and that his rights will be protected at that even if I should talk to you about lands, and the selling of them, it is not true that soldiers are coming here to take them by force. I am told that even now some of you want to make a treaty about lands. If it be so, I do not think we could agree now. My plans might not suit me.

"We want more time to think of it, than we have now. When you want to talk about your lands, by and by, I shall be ready to talk," Stevens concluded.

The tribe chose Garry to represent them. He was to inform Stevens they were not ready for a reservation.

"What I have in my heart I will speak out, after I have spoken you will know my mind. Now they are fighting among the Yakimas, and it is on my mind all the time. When we heard this news from the Yakimas, it troubled us some, but still we are not like them. When I heard of the war, I had two hearts, and have had had two hearts ever since. I had two hearts; the bad heart was a little larger than the good. The war is now there [here Garry pointed to the west] what can we do now you are going down the country, to have our people always good. (Lewis)

"Since I heard of trouble among the Indians, I have had you on my mind all the time. It is Peace I want. Now I am thinking that if you do not make peace with the Yakimas, war will come into this Country like the waters of the sea.

"From the time of my first recollection, no blood has ever been upon the hands of my people. Now that I am grown up, I am

86

afraid that we may have the blood of the Whites on our hands. I don't like that." [Garry paused and then turned and looked straight at Stevens.] "I told you at the Walla Walla Council that we do not wish to turn our arms against the Whites. My heart is that way, but my eyes look further. I have told all my men to keep quiet; it will be so as you think."

"I would not like it is the troops should come to the junction of the Columbia and Snake rivers-- I would not like to have the Yakimas driven this way. The women and children would be too much trouble. If the troops come over this way my family and people will not be able to get their roots, and will be troubled.

"You may say you want peace here, I am glad. I hope also you will make peace on the other side of the Columbia, and keep the soldiers from coming here. The Americans and the Yakima's are fighting. I think they are both equally guilty. Now if you will make peace, I shall be very glad.

"If there were many Frenchmen here, my heart would be like fighting. We had before you came, been talking about our lands, these French people have talked too much. [Garry motioned towards the settlers, with the wave of a hand.] I hope they will shut up their mouths. I will never hide my mind, what I think I will speak out.

"Now if my heart were weak, you would put me in trouble by your talk. If my heart were weak, the whites about here might have put me in trouble by their talk about the land, I think that you French people [Garry turned and addressed himself to a number of white settlers present,] will not talk any more about the land, that now you will be done. Now you Frenchmen, listen to the Governor; listen to the chiefs, and when a Treaty is made, then talk about your lands.

"I was absent from here, I went to the Walla Walla Treaty, and when I returned I found that all the Frenchmen had got their lands written down in a paper by Judge Yantis (Garry was alluding to the notifications of the taking of claims under the Donations Law which he settlers had prepared for forwarding to the Surveyor General's Office).

Raising his voice he asked the settlers,"Why are you in such a hurry to have writings for your lands now? Why are you in such a hurry? Why don't you wait until the Treaty is made? Then you will have your lands. Whether it belongs to the Indians or to the Government, you will have your lands.

[Garry turned to face Stevens again, and went on.] "The Indians and French about here are always telling the Whites lies about Garry. Now I will speak for myself, I am an Indian, I was the first one to spill my blood for the whites in the Spanish Country, and afterwards when blood was spilled in the Cayuse Country.

"The Indians are always thinking of this—of an Indian, who was killed in California by an American (Note-meaning Elijah, Peupeumoxmox's son who was shot down in cold blood).

"A white man was the cause of Whitman's death. A white man in the employ of Dr. Whitman carried false reports to the Indians' camp. Not long after that, war was made upon the Cayuse's for the murderers, and they were given up.

"Governor, I will not hide my mind. Those troubles are on my mind all the time and I will not hide them. When I was at the Cayuse Treaty, my mind was divided. When you commenced the Treaty, the Interpreters were all sworn on the book to tell the truth. I was glad of it. You spoke on nine different things during three days and I was looking on what you spoke. When you had spoken on these nine different things, then you asked the Chiefs to speak. The Chiefs spoke and you answered in one word. My heart thought that word was bad.

"When you first commenced to speak, you said the Walla Wallas, Cayuses, and Umatillas were to move onto the Nez Perce Reservation, and that the Spokanes were to move there also. Then I thought you spoke bad. Then I thought you said that, you would strike the Indian to the heart.

"After you had spoken of those nine different things, as schools and farms, and shops, if you had then asked the Chiefs to mark out a piece of land-a pretty large piece-to give you, it would not have struck the Indians so to the heart. Your thought was good, you see far, but the Indians being dull-headed cannot see far-that is why I thought it would strike their hearts.

"This that I have shown you is my heart. I have in my mind what I am saying now. Now your children are fallen, they have spilled their blood, because they have not sense enough to understand you.

"Those who killed Peupeumoxmox's son, in California, they are Americans, Why are those three Americans alive now? Why are they not hung? This is what the Indians think, that it will be Indians only who are hung for murder.

"Now Governor, here are these young people--my people-- I do not know their minds, but if they will listen, I shall be very glad.

"When you talk to your soldiers and tell them not to cross the Snake River into our country, I shall be glad.

"Tomorrow after breakfast, I hope you will know the hearts of all these chiefs present."

Garry stated the grievances of the Indians that disturbed them: French Canadian encroachment, the outcome of the Walla Walla Council, Steven's actions, the murder of Elijah Hedding, and the Yakima War. He told his people the soldiers were peaceful, but they did not believe him, alarmed at the U.S. Army column being so far east of the route to Fort Colville. Garry believed in keeping peace with the young braves in the village, but his influence suffered. He did not want to make war with them. His speech put Stevens on the defensive.

Garry's tribe nodded in assent and spoke out in approval following his speech. They recognized that Spokane Garry had a grasp of the situation. Stevens made a speech to win Garry over.

"The Chief Garry has spoken from his heart. He has spoken boldly, and spoken frankly. That is good, I like it. I have known Garry a long time. Garry has been with me in my house for weeks.

"I met Garry as he says at the Walla Walla Council. What Garry said as to what I said is right. I did say it. I asked Garry would his people like to go to the Nez Perce Reservation? Would they be satisfied there?" Garry said, "I have not asked my people; but when I get home I will ask them." Stevens continued...

"I said to Garry, when I get to see your people I will talk with them and see what arrangements can be made about it. I never said to Garry, though your people shall be moved to the Nez Perce River. If Garry's people were willing to go, I would like it, that was what I said, and Garry was sorry, because he felt that his people would not like it.

"I have not come here to urge upon you the sale of your lands. I have not come to talk about that unless you wish it. I think it is better for you that your minds be settled and quieted. I want you to feel that I am your friend, and that I will protect every Indian, so far as I have means and strength. We have laws for punishing white men who do wrong to Indians. Those laws are put in force.

"I will explain a little, Garry has been there, he knows where I live. There Indians work a good deal for white men in mills and on farms. I have had Indians come to me and say, 'I worked for this man a month and he won't pay me,' and in every case I have got the Indians paid, except in one case, where the man went off in a vessel.

"Garry has referred to Peupeumoxmox's son who was killed in California. His name was Elijah. He was a man whom the Americans of Oregon loved. He was a good man and ever the friend of the Whites. The Americans who lived there, pitied and grieved for his death, and for Peupeumoxmox. At that time things were very much unsettled in California, and it was difficult to arrest or punish any man for murder.

"Garry knows that in San Francisco they could [not] convict the worst white man for murder or any other crime. Garry knows that the people had to rise up and seize the murderers and hang them, because the Courts would not do it. Since then the times have changed and the white man has been hanged for killing Indians." Governor Stevens then asserted that Chiefs Kamiakin and Peupeumoxmox had signed the treaty that he made that would protect the Indians. In conclusion Stevens added,

"I can only say to Garry, that with the Indians who are friendly, we can get along. Garry and myself can do our own business together with the Spokanes and Coeur d' Alenes and Colvilles. I have no more to say tonight. We will talk tomorrow as Garry has said, and then I want all to speak boldly and frankly as Garry has done."

The Indians must have discussed what they would say the next day, and Stevens and his advisors must have too.

Wednesday, the 5th of December, the tribal council resumed at ten o'clock that morning. Nine Indians spoke in succession, representing the three tribes and spoke of peace and friendship with the whites. An Indian objected to the white man coming, some with smallpox. Another asked why Governor Stevens had stopped the Hudson's Bay Company from selling ammunition to the Indians which was so desperately needed for them to hunt. No Indian suggested a treaty giving land to the white man.

The Spokane tribe chose Garry to represent them, which he later did. Resentment caused by the white man's arrogance toward the Indians and Steven's manner in the council at Walla Walla, Spokane Garry knowing the support backing him, communicated directly to Stevens. Garry stood before him and spoke.

"Governor, see the difference there is between these Indians and you. See how everybody is red and you are white. The Indians think they are not poor. When you look at yourself, you see you are white. You see the Indian is red, what do you think? Do you think they are poor when you look at them that way? When you look at those red men, you think you have more heart, more sense than those poor Indians. I think the difference between us and you Americans is in the clothing; the blood and body are the same." "Do you think because your mother was white, and theirs black that you are higher or better? We are black, yet if we cut ourselves, the blood will be red-and so with the whites it is the same, though their skin is white. I do not think we are poor, because we belong to another nation. I am of another nation, when I speak you do not understand me. When you speak, I do not understand you.

"Today Governor, we meet together. You say you want to know my heart and that is the reason we are talking for nothing. Now you take those Indians here for chiefs. Do you think it? If you believe what they say, it is all right. If you take those Indians for men, treat them so now. The Indians are proud, they are not poor. If you talk truth to the Indians to make a peace, the Indians will do the same for you. You now see the Indians are proud.

"On account of one of your remarks some of your people have already fallen on the ground. The Indians are not satisfied with the land you gave them. What commenced the trouble was the murder of Peupeumoxmox's son, and Dr. Whitman, and now they find their Reservation too small.

"If all those Indians had marked out their own Reservation, this trouble would not have happened. I am thinking always of that. No doubt your White people are thinking the same. We are down-hearted and you are.

"Governor, you want to know all the Indians' hearts, we are going to tell the truth on each side. You want to know the hearts of the Indians and they want to know yours. You want to take the Indians for Indians, and not hide your mind from them. If your heart is true, show it to the Indians and all will be right. I am showing my heart that you may see it.

"Now the Indians are in trouble. If you could get their Reservation made a little larger, they would be pleased-this is my mind, but perhaps it is too late to do it. For myself, I am an Indian. If I had the business to do, I could fix it by giving them a little more land. Talking about land I am only telling you my mind. What I said yesterday about not crossing the soldiers to this side of the Columbia is my business. Those Indians have gone to war, and I don't know myself how to fix it up again. That is your business.

"Since Governor, the beginning of the world, there has been war. Why cannot you manage to keep the peace? Maybe there will be no peace ever. Even if you should have all the bad people, war could begin again, and would never stop."

War was raging in the west, to the south in Oregon, in Yakima and in Walla Walla country. The Spokanes were neutral. Garry wrote to Governor Stevens saying that the Spokanes and probably the Cayuses would not join the hostiles. At the time, the peaceful Spokane prospered and traded goods to the Hudson's Bay Company at Fort Colville for supplies. Spokane horse and cattle herds had increased to a surplus. The Spokane fished for salmon and liked their Reservation, as did the Cayuse, Umatillas and Walla Wallas. The Indians present doubted his statement, since the Cayuse and Walla Walla were on the war trail.

Group Photo, Chief Garry,
Second from Right, First Row
Public Domain

Stevens spoke. "Have you anything further that you wish to speak about? Do you want to speak about lands? Do you wish to point out lands you want the whites to have? I call on Garry to answer."

Garry would have rather heard that the tribes were assured of retaining their ancestral lands. He knew his people would have a hard time accepting the treaty that would give their lands to the whites without permission and open it up for settlement. Indians found it more convenient to put off at the time.

He answered the Governor. "All these things we have been speaking of had better be tied together as they are, like a bundle of sticks, because you are in a hurry. There is not time to talk of them. But afterwards you can come back, when you find time and see us." Stevens remained silent.

Garry, representing the Coeur d'Alene, Colville, and Spokane tribes, had accomplished what no other tribe in the territory had. He blocked Stevens from taking their lands for the white man.

In 1856, Garry received a letter from Governor Stevens requesting the Cayuse, Nez Perce, Walla Walla, and Umatilla tribes for another treaty council.

Gary knew these tribes were hostile and did not wish to go so he wrote Stevens a letter. He told him that he could not attend because it was salmon season and they had the great task of putting up the fish as salmon is the only food that they could store up for the winter.

Garry had foreseen the council to be a failure and said the Stevens party was lucky to get out of hostile Indian Territory alive. Warriors had attacked them, but they joined forces with the troops at Fort Walla Walla. The combined forces retreated to the west at Fort Dalles. General John Ellis Wood ordered that the region west of the Cascades be cleared of all white settlers.

Coeur d'Alene Indian Warriors Acting Out
Photo Courtesy of Azusa Publishing, LLC

Spokane Women
At Work
Public Domain

General J. Steptoe
Photo Courtesy of Wikipedia.org

# CHAPTER NINE
## THE STEPTOE WAR

Garry had urged the soldiers to stay south of the Snake River, as not to incite his young warriors, but in 1858, Colonel E. J. Steptoe's command crossed the Snake River toward Rosalia and Steptoe Butte where Garry's Spokane and other tribes were gathering Camas roots in the spring. Garry tried to intervene and voice his opinion that the whole tribe should not have to pay for what a few warriors did. Stevens, hearing of the Spokane uprising, demanded to speak with Garry. After the council, Stevens said he just wanted to consult with the Coeur d' Alenes and Spokanes about where they might be moved. He would take their wishes into consideration since they had "given me their hearts about it." (Ruby and Brown)

April of 1858, Steptoe got a petition from settlers at Fort Colville seeking protection from Indians who had murdered two whites and stolen cattle. He recommended a foray to impress the Indians of their military power. In the spring of 1858, Steptoe moved his troops from Fort Walla-Walla into Spokane Territory.

When Lt. Col. Steptoe arrived at Fort Vancouver the Indians demanded to know his intentions; Chief Spokane Garry, Christian Indian, diplomat, spokesman, teacher, and peace chief, friend to Indian and white man did not understand why the Army came and stopped by to talk with Steptoe and asked the colonel why they were there? The colonel said they meant them no harm.

The Indians were peaceful, but refused their use of canoes to cross the Spokane River blocking their advance to Ft. Colville. Troops under Colonel Edward Steptoe left Fort Walla Walla, with several Nez Perce scouts in the spring of 1858 to investigate the murder of two gold miners in the Fort Colville area a few miles north of the Spokane River. The Steptoe campaign had not suspected problems with the Indian Tribes living north of the

Snake River. Col. Steptoe thought that he could intimidate the Coeur d'Alene Indians with a show of government force, but they didn't appreciate him riding through Indian lands.

The Indians besieged by farmers, fur traders, miners, and ranchers were ready to fight, but Nez Perce Chief Timothy assisted Steptoe and troops in crossing the Snake River at Horse-Alpowa Creek. Steptoe was again aided crossing the Snake. After the council, Stevens said that he only wanted to consult with the Coeur d'Alene and Spokane about where they might be moved. He would take their wishes into consideration.

Some riled up Spokane braves rode out on the war path. Lewis described the Spokane 'head men,' who tried to prevent the wild young braves from going to war. "Spokane chiefs succeeded for a time in holding us, but soon the warriors went galloping off to fight. They joined the Coeur d'Alene in war." Garry wrote, "They would not listen to me, but the boys shot at him; I was very sorry."

A fight broke out May 17, 1858, when the Coeur d'Alene, Colville, Columbia River, Kalispell, and Spokane Indians attacked. a column of U.S. Army regulars under Lt. Colonel Edward Steptoe from Fort Colville at the Tohotonimme, they were inadequately armed with older muzzle-loading rifles, hard to load on horseback. Officers carried Colt Dragoon revolvers and forty rounds per man. When Lt. Colonel led 152 enlisted men, five officers and two other officers, totaling 160 men, thirty volunteers, a pack train and three Nez Perce scouts into combat, the battle raged! Still, the Army lost seven soldiers, in the fray.

Steptoe had made bad choices. A war party of painted Indians taunted the soldiers. War cries filled the air. The column moved past the creek tributary into a draw between two hills. Garry had gotten his crops in, when he received word to join a delegation of tribal chiefs of the Colville, Coeur d'Alene, Flathead, Kalispell, and Spokane. Garry declined since it was salmon season.

Steptoe had retreated to Fort Colville the next day. The command rose at dawn and rode back to Pine Creek. Jesuit missionary, Father Joseph Joset tried to intervene and defuse the fighting. The soldiers pressed ahead holding their fire. Bullets began striking the troops. The Indians cut them off, dividing the unit in two. They counter-attacked to avoid being surrounded. Two officers were killed; during the fighting the rest of the troops formed a circle ducking behind pack animals, saving them.

In 1858, Garry released his anger in a letter to Governor Stevens and General Newman S. Clarke, regional commander. He said Stevens had "broke the hearts of all Indians" by his suggestion that they go to the Nez Perce and Yakima lands and said that it would have been alright if Stevens had given the Indians the decision of what portion of the lands to give.

"I am sorry that the war has begun," wrote Garry. "Like a fire in a dry prairie, it will spread all over the country, until now so peaceful. I hear already from different parts rumors of other Indians ready to take in. Make peace and the American soldiers may go about; we don't care. That's my own private opinion."

Garry

The Army ordered Col. George Wright in the fall of 1858 to punish the Indians for Steptoe's defeat; Wright penetrated deep into the heart of Spokane country. At the Battle of the Four Lakes, Colonel Wright defeated the Spokane warriors between Spokane and Cheney, Washington. Wright again defeated the Spokane, two days later at the Battle of the Spokane Plains.

Garry did not join the fighting and had gone to Fort Colville for supplies at the time, but felt deeply troubled about the events. He told a doctor at Fort Colville, "My heart is undecided; I do not know which way to go. My friends are fighting the whites. I do not like to join them, but if I do not they will kill me."

101

George Wright's Retaliation into Spokane Country
Photo Courtesy of Wikipedia.org

September 1, 1858, Col. George Wright came for revenge leading a column of 600 Dragoons in hot pursuit of the Indians through Spokane Valley, burning fields of grain, dried fruit, and vegetables. September 9, Col. Wright found 800 head of the tribes' mustangs near Liberty Lake, captured 100 ponies and butchered the rest to render the Indians powerless, and needlessly killing all of the tribe's horses. "They kill the horses, don't they?"

The Battle of Four Lakes occurred on September 5, 1858 about 15 miles south of Spokane Falls, where Wright's Army encountered a huge band of hostile Indian ready for a fight. They were armed with bows and arrows, lances, and muskets. The Army was equipped with new long rifles having a 600 yard range. The Indians carried old Hudson's Bay muskets only with a 200 yard range. The Indians charged and rode off repeating the maneuver again. Warriors attacked and wheeled to attack again. The Indians fired the prairie grass behind them and the wind carried the smoke and flame making it hard to breath, but the soldiers rode through the smoke and ash. Wright had a decisive victory. Eighteen to twenty Indians were shot dead before they retreated.

At the Battle of the Spokane Plains Wrights Army fought 500-700 Coeur d'Alene, Palouse, Pend d' Oreille, and Spokane warriors. They charged and emitted loud war whoops, wheeling and returning to fight. Using fires, they fought bravely, yet no Americans were slain, two of Garry's brothers died in the battle.

Chief Spokane Garry and another prominent chief, named Big Star met with Colonel Wright a few weeks later on September 23, 1858 on Latah Creek and signed a peace treaty, which was more of a surrender. Wright sent word for the tribes to meet at Smyth's Ford on Latah Creek, September 24, 1858. Seven chiefs from the Palouse, Pend d' Oreille, Coleville, and Spokane tribes were present. Wright told them they must let the white man cross their land or be hunted down. Settlers flooded Indian lands.

"I have heard that the Nez Perce were talking of war." Garry wrote, "That makes me uneasy and study much; for my part I don't like to see them take up their arms, for they will gain nothing by it. I have heard that you talk hard about us, by Indians, but I don't believe it; but I think it is all the Yakima's doing, to get us to join them, but I don't believe it, for they want me to go to war by all means; but I would rather be quiet."

Garry

Garry could sense his people's anguish and avoided important decisions, but he had been selected to be spokesman of the tribes. Delivering a long passionate speech revealed the Indian viewpoint and listed their concerns: the Yakima War, the murder of Elijah Hedding, the Whitman Massacre, and the Indian agent's attitude at the treaty councils. The speech left Stevens defensive; it was the first time talks with Spokane failed to produce a treaty.

The Spokane warriors, who fought in the battle, rode to the Upper Missouri for the buffalo hunt and returned to camp. Garry called a tribal council and spoke of petitioning the government for peace, asking for an Indian agent, accepting a treaty and permitting military roads across their territory.

Garry's Spokanes suffered a long, hard winter of 1858-59, after Colonel Wright destroyed all of the tribe's caches food and grain stores.

The winter of 1859-1960, Garry carried the mail between Spokane Territory and Fort Benton, Montana. Although Garry rode horses, he had to resort to snowshoes at times. As a stroke of luck, Garry's provisions were missed by Wright's soldiers. He attempted to assist the Middle and Upper Spokane to survive the winter doing trading with Fort Colville. Chief Big Head of the Lower Spokane tribe died during that period removing some of the completion with Garry. As soon as Garry's crops were in, he was called to Walla Walla and Vancouver to see the military authorities. Garry was asked to send a horse to Chief Kamiakin to ride to Walla Walla to join them, but he could not attend.

Months after the treaty, on March 28, 1859, Garry arrived in Walla Walla and petitioned the U.S. government for peace in the presence of Indian agent A. G. Cain and wrote W.S. Harney, Commander of the Department of Oregon and Washington at Fort Vancouver. His letter read.

"Sir: my people are desirous of having peace with the whites. Their wish is to have an Indian agent and soldiers live in this country to protect them. All of the chiefs and all of the people are ready and willing to make a treaty with the government for the sale of their lands. They are perfectly satisfied with having roads made through their country. For myself, if a 'treaty' is made with us for our lands, I wish our reservation to be located where we will not be interrupted by the whites. We have so many dishonest men who would steal from the whites, if they were near them that it would occasion much trouble. My horses have given out, and it is so late in the spring I will have to return home to attend to my crops, or I would go and see you. If you should visit here this spring the Indian agent will send me word, and I will come down and see you. I have the honor to be, very respectfully, your most obedient servant,"

SPOKAN GARRY

Garry's letter was forwarded to Army headquarters with the following comment, "In justice to the Indians, this should be adopted by our government; they already cultivate the soil in part for subsistence and, unless protected in their right to do so, they will be forced into miserable warfare until they are exterminated."

The delegation of Colville, Coeur d'Alene, Flathead, Kalispell, and Spokane Indian chiefs met on May 30, 1859. Brigadier General Harney warned the chiefs to behave or he would unleash his troops on the tribes. The chiefs were shown the U.S. Army's military might and then were taken on tour through the states of Oregon and Washington demonstrating their agriculture, houses of commerce, and food sources.

Garry could see that it was not a good idea for the Indians to go to war with the white man. He had seen their might and knew their strength in number.

In 1860, Congress passed the Homestead Act, legislation that entitled settlers to assume 160 acres of Indian land and to work it as their own. Stevens proposed that the Spokane sell off its lands and move onto the reservation shared by the Nez Perce or Yakima tribes.

Garry worked as a guide on the Snake River for his friend, Major John Owen. The major often visited Garry at home. In 1867, when Garry returned from the buffalo hunt, he dictated a letter to a friend for J.R. Bates Spokane County state legislature. It read:

"Dear Sir, Last fall, I left the Spokane's for the buffalo country and have just returned to my home. I left part of my family on the road coming down. It is my intention to go back immediately for them with fresh horses. I will be back right away if my son and daughter are all right; which will be in a week and I may be gone a month or more if anything else shall have happened there. My object in writing to you at this time is to say to you that I am ready at any time now when I am at home to make a treaty; but I don't want anything done during my absence. It is with a view to a full understanding of matters that I address you this note."

Garry

Garry spoke to the Spokane and described all their grievances and their unwillingness to give up ancestral lands. "When I heard of the war, I had two hearts and have had two hearts ever since. I had two hearts. The bad heart is a little larger than the good." Stevens knew they would not sell.

Garry told Stevens, "When you first commenced to speak, you said the Walla Walla's, and the Umatilla's were to move onto the Nez Perce reservation and the Spokane was to move there, also. Then, I thought you spoke bad. Then I thought you would strike the Indians to the heart." Stevens was taken aback, knowing it was but a proposal as the council session ended.

Although some furs were traded at the post, it acted as a central location for the Hudson's Bay administration office, in 1869, the HBC surrendered its monopoly in the northwest to the North West Company. The fort was seized in early 1870 by Louis Rieland and his Metis during the Red River Rebellion.

In 1872, the Colville Reservation was established by executive order of President Ulysses S. Grant for the Colville, Chelan, Coeur d'Alene, Entiat, Kalispell, Lakes, Methow, Nespelem, Okanagan, Palouse, Sanpoil, Spokane, Southern Okanagan, and Wenatchee tribes. Some Spokane Indians did finally settle at Fort Colville Indian reservation.

Garry wrote to as many officials as possible. Garry's ideas were sometimes accepted or rejected, never reaching fruition. Garry met with the Commandant of the Department of the Columbia and was told the government had no interest in giving them a reservation and not to cause trouble.

In 1877, the government warned of moving the Spokane to a reservation on the Columbia. Garry's replied, "What right do you have to dictate to us? This is our country and we will not leave it."

Howard described Garry in an insulting manner. "Spokane Garry was short in stature, dressed in citizen's clothing, and wore his hair cut short for an Indian. He was shriveled, bleary eyed and repulsive in appearance, but wiry and tough and still able to endure great fatigue, though he must have been at least 70 years in age."

End Note: Garry's treaty speeches: pg. 83-107 "Chief Spokan Garry," Thomas E. Jesset

Garry had succeeded in preventing Governor Stevens from assigning them to the reservation and keeping the government from taking the Spokans' land. At the same time, Garry tried to keep the peace following the Treaty of Walla Walla.

On the morning of June 17, 1877, U.S. Army Captain Perry and two companies of troops, volunteers, and scouts rode down into White Bird Canyon in Idaho Territory. They were met by peaceful Nez Perce Indian warriors bearing a white flag. Suddenly, a rifle crack broke the silence, then another striking the dirt next to the warriors. Ad Chapman, a foolish scout started it.

The Nez Perce warriors returned fire and the Nez Perce War had begun. The Indians stripped down into war shirts, loin cloths, and moccasins, ready for war. The Army suffered defeat that day. Chief Joseph retreated trying to reach Canada in a running fight with the Army.

Early in 1877, some Middle Spokane Indians were digging camas roots near Farmington, Washington, when they heard that the Nez Perce tribe had gone on the warpath. A messenger was sent to the white man at Spokane Falls that assured them the Spokane had no intention of warring.

Fearing attack, a stockade for protection from the Indians was erected. Hostile Nez Perce warriors taunted the Spokane trying to join them before departing, but Garry had no intention of going on the war trail and he advised his warriors to do the same.

Chief Spokan Garry had been and always would be a peace chief. He was civilized and lived a Christian life. Chief Garry was a man of his word. Unfortunately, his two brothers died in battle, which grieved Garry deeply. He had done so much to keep peace between the Spokane and the white man. Although he hit bottom once in his life, Garry pulled himself up. His home and land were stolen from him and he died in poverty, but the bright career of a very influential man was recognized for his accomplishments.

Steptoe Butte
Public Domain

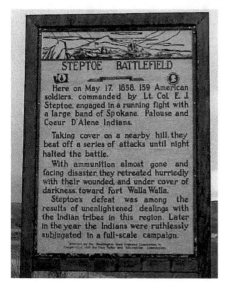

STEPTOE BATTLEFIELD

Here on May 17, 1858, 159 American soldiers, commanded by Lt. Col E. J. Steptoe, engaged in a running fight with a large band of Spokane, Palouse and Coeur D'Alene Indians.

Taking cover on a nearby hill, they beat off a series of attacks until night halted the battle.

With ammunition almost gone and facing disaster, they retreated hurriedly with their wounded, and under cover of darkness, toward Fort Walla Walla.

Steptoe's defeat was among the results of unenlightened dealings with the Indian tribes in this region. Later in the year the Indians were ruthlessly subjugated in a full-scale campaign.

BATTLE
OF
FOUR LAKES

ON THIS HISTORIC GROUND, SEPT. 1, 1858, 700 SOLDIERS UNDER COL. GEO. WRIGHT, U.S.A. ROUTED 5000 ALLIED INDIANS.

FOUR DAYS LATER THE RALLIED HOSTILES WERE DECISIVELY DEFEATED IN A RUNNING BATTLE. THEY SUED FOR MERCY, AND HAVE EVER SINCE MAINTAINED LASTING PEACE

ERECTED BY
Spokane County Pioneer Society
Medical Lake Commercial Club
Four Lakes Grange

1935

Steptoe Battle Monument
Photo Courtesy of Azusa
Publishing, LLC

Battle of Four Lakes
Public Domain

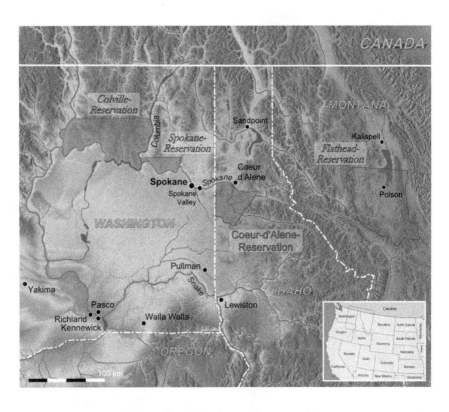

Map of the Spokane Reservation
Photo Courtesy of Wikipedia.org

# CHAPTER TEN
## THE SPOKANE INDIAN
## RESERVATION

Spokane ancestors of the tribe were people of the Plateau, who shared cultural traits with neighboring tribes for hundreds of years, dwelling along the Spokane River. The Spokane fished, hunted and gathered in seasonal rounds. The Spokane shared their language with other tribes in the region: the Coeur d'Alene, Colville, Flathead and Kalispell. The Spokane was composed of the Lower, Middle, and Upper Bands.

Garry dedicated his life to serve as liaison between the U.S. Army and his tribe. In return, He asked only that his tribe be able to have their reservation on ancestral grounds on both sides of the Spokane River where he designated adjusting to the palefaces, but was turned down. Instead traditional lands were taken away and they were confined to a small reservation of the government's choosing or by use of the Homestead Act, expecting them to take up land claims and Indian Homesteads if natives gave up tribal annuities, exemptions, and privileges until they got a reservation.

The Indians were forced to relinquish and sell millions of acres of their ancestral lands to the government, which were given to the white settlers. The Spokanes did not receive gifts from the government, only a few supplies from Fort Colville. Life as they had known it was fleeting. Garry and the Spokane were running out of time. The government stalled over a Spokane reservation.

On August 10th, ten companies of federal troops arrived at Spokane Falls and a council was called of Coeur d'Alene, Colville, Spokane, and other close tribes numbering three thousand. At the council, a reservation was proposed for the Spokane Indians. The reservation was to span from Chimokan Creek in Washington territory down to the Spokane River, to the Columbia River, to the mouth of the Minchen Creek. The land was not fertile the pasture land was poor, as was the fishing. The reservation became known as Watkins Reservation, after U.S. Indian agent, George E.C. Watkins, who proposed a six mile stretch of land of the Columbia River from the mouth of the Kettle River to the Spokane River be added to expand the size of the reservation. In August of 1877, the Lower Spokane band relocated to the Spokane Reservation.

In 1879, during a council meeting, Garry argued for a reservation that would be adequate for his people. Howard was impressed by him and said that Garry showed himself more of a lawyer than a warrior." and General O.O. Howard said that Garry spoke like a lawyer and "knew how to filibuster like a congressman" (Lewis) They came to no agreement, and agreed to meet again. The Spokane returned to their homes.

A council met on October 20, 1880 with Colonel W.J. Pollock, U.S. Indian Inspector, who urged the Spokane to take homesteads or transition onto reservations and went on to explain that the railroad would soon reach Spokane Falls. Indian farmers were opposed to the reserves and were expected to apply for Indian Homesteads, but they did not desire to sever relations with the rest of the tribe and it was hard for them to raise the $22.00 filing fees.

In January 18, 1881, President Rutherford B. Hayes declared the Spokane Indian Reservation as part of the Colville Agency to be the new home of the Spokanes. The edge of the reserve began where the Chemakane Creek crosses the 48 degrees down the east bank of the creek to where it enters the Spokane River, westward to the confluence with the Columbia, then eastward to the starting point. The Spokane reservation lies on traditional lands bounded on the south by the Spokane River and the west by the Columbia in eastern Washington. The reservation sprawls over 157,000 acres; 90% of the reservation held in trust by the federal government. Originally, Spokane Territory spanned over 3,000,000 acres of land.

Sam Psone- George McCrae- Robert Flett- Fred Finch- Herman Boyd-
John LeBert- Paul Elyah- John Sherwood- Glenn Galbraith- Iva LeBert-
Rosa Wynecoop- Milan Taudy- Gertrude Galbraith- Cora Taudy- Lillian
LeBert- Gertrude Flett- Ida Psone- Marjorie Smith - Harold Troit.

Indians on Spokane Reservation
Photo Courtesy of Wikipedia.org

The reserve was small and a disappointment to the Indians and the Indian Agent. Only the Lower Spokane lived there. One resident was Nellie, Garry's daughter from the marriage to Lucy, his first wife, who must have passed by then. The Spokane Reservation was two very small parcels of land that totalled 1.5 acres and part of the Spokane River in the northwestern United States in eastern Washington State.

In 1881, Garry's Upper Spokanes agreed to move to Colville; 3 bands of the tribe were split up and found homes on the Coeur d'Alene, Colville and Flathead Indian Reservations. In 1881, the railroad arrived in Spokane Falls.

In 1882, the Dawes Commission was formed in Spokane Falls in order to try and dissuade the Coeur d'Alene and Spokane Indians to transition onto reservations. Garry met with the U.S. Army as mediator along the Spokane River. Army blankets were spread on the ground so the chiefs and sub-chiefs could sit cross-legged under a large tent. Both tribes were represented. Garry, late for the talks rode in on a beautiful white horse wearing an eagle-feather war bonnet, a stylish, white buckskin outfit, moccasins, and carried a marvelous bow and quiver of arrows.

Garry did not enter the tent, but remained on his horse. He was terribly bow-legged, possibly from scurvy as a child, barrel-chested and short-legged, making him self-conscious. Garry took command and initiated the council meeting without waiting for the Commissioners. He was the only chief that spoke fluent English, having been educated at the Red River Mission in Canada. Using sign language, the Salish dialect, and English Garry spoke for his tribe as one of the greatest American Indian orators. He noted the wrong doings of the white man and the need for a reservation. Garry complained the white man had taken the Spokane River, "the mother of his people," at her breast for nourishment and the salmon the main source of food for them.

Flathead Indian Reservation
Photo Courtesy of Wikipedia.org

In 1882, Garry noted that the gold miners were stealing Spokane Falls for the valuable gold stones in the rapid water and wanted the falls. The settlers were pouring into the valley never ending. Garry explained that they were too many to try and stop.

Garry described to the council the Battle of Four Lakes, when General Wright defeated the tribes. He explained how he had tried to prevent the young warriors from going on the war trail. Then Garry explained how General Wright had discovered the tribe's 800 horses by the lake and had slaughtered them all near the Spokane Bridge. The Indians escaped on foot into the mountains. The salmon were running yet they had no horses to complete their food cycle. General Wright gave the Spokane dried beans, flour and salt pork to tide them over.

Garry requested a reservation in 1887 on both sides of the Spokane River for 20 miles for the Middle and Upper Spokane; it was denied. Garry finally got his treaty, but no reservation. Garry swore he would not enter the reserve and allow the palefaces to take their lands and said he would die first, his bones buried in the land of his ancestors. He took off his war bonnet and spoke, "I have sworn this on the headdress of my father and my father's father." He took the reins turning his horse toward home.

In 1887, after days of talks in the last council meeting, an agreement was made in writing between the Spokane and government officials. Chief Garry and 92 elders ceded all of their lands, 314 million acres to the United States for $80,000, the equivalent of $.32 per acre and agreed to move onto the Coeur d'Alene, Colville, or Jocko reservations. They were to be given lieu lands among the Coeur d'Alene Indians and the government agreed to pay $90.00 for building homes and the surroundings; every Indian that formed five acres of land received $5,000.00 from the government. Garry and other chiefs were promised $100.00 for over ten years.

Colville Indian Family
Photo Courtesy of Wikipedia.org

He pressed for a reserve by the Spokane River, but was denied. The agreement was ratified by Congress March 15, 1887 and 92 Indians made their mark. The Middle Spokane band agreed to move to the Colville Reservation. Today the Spokane Reservation is about 159,000 acres. The tribe has 2708 tribal members and growing. It consists of 108,874 acres of forest land, 8,552 acres of agricultural land, and 10,328 acres of lakes with 25 maintained camp sites. There was a promotion to rectify the Spokane Kalispell dialect in language schools and immersion programs on the reservation. One class targeted children ages three to eight. The school has free classes in the Spokane dialect as their language continues. The Spokane House became a boarding school for the children of the Spokane Tribe from 1898-1906 and 651 members of the tribe received $64,750 allotted in individual plots.

In 1933, after Garry's death construction began on the Grand Coulee Dam on the Columbia in central Washington, 90 miles west of Spokane. It was 550 feet high and 500 feet wide at the base ending salmon migration and Spokane's fishery; the buffalo and beaver were gone. Water rose 400 feet flooding tribal lands. Lake Roosevelt rose 70 feet. Columbia River Gorge has numerous lakes and tributaries, taking in the Snake River.

The Spokanes dwelled in eastern Washington at Wellpinit on the Spokane Indian Reservation and at the Tribal Headquarters in Stevens County; this included two small parcels of land in Lincoln County encompassing part of the Spokane River. Wellpinit is around 50 miles northwest of Spokane. The reservation spans 237 square miles. Spokane members on the reservation number approximately 2,000 people according to the U.S. Census. The Spokane lands once reached over three million acres of land. Uranium was discovered in the 1930's and mined in 1956-1962 from open pits and from 1969-1982 by the Midnight Mine.

# CHAPTER ELEVEN
## TRAILS END

Missionaries came early. Settlers came west in Conestoga wagons after 1842 along the Oregon Trail. Gold miners arrived after 1849. After the Civil War, President Lincoln sent soldiers west to protect the settlers. Settlers arrived by the thousands and were pushing the Indians off their lands and Garry believed in living on the land and not on the reservation. He had his farm at the foot of a hill. Laws read that the land Garry farmed was legally his as long as he improved it. He tried to negotiate the Indians living in white man's territory, but the government never agreed.

In 1888, Garry took his family to a fishing camp of the Spokane along the Spokane River. Summer fishing camps were popular fisheries. Oblong Fishing huts were grouped together providing defense from attack. While at the fishing camp, Garry got word that his farm had been taken over by a white trespasser.

He rushed home and found that Schyler D. Doak, a land grabber, had assumed his property. He told Garry to keep off his land, maybe at gunpoint. Garry decided to evict him by legal means. The Treaty of 1887 was to protect the natives by the Indian Homestead Act and Garry believed land along the Spokane River belonged to the Indians, but was forced to vacate his land. He had worked hard to till the land and fenced it off in order to live there.

With no other choice, but to leave, Garry loaded most of his possessions and farm equipment. It took more than one trip to empty the log storehouse on his farm, but when he returned he found that the trespasser had burned the cabin to the ground. He said he couldn't wait because he wanted to plow the field.

Luckily, Garry was able to salvage his Bible and Common Book of Prayer. The trespasser evicted Garry and drove him from his farm near Hillyard in Spokane. He had no choice but to revert back to tipi living, forced to move off his land unable to secure

Garry's Teepee
Wife, Horse and Dogs
Public Domain

more; his situation went from bad to worse. He and his relatives set up teepees on the second bench west of Hangman Creek [where hostile Yakima Chief Qualchien had been hanged September 24, 1858]. Colonel Wright hung eight more hostiles. Garry and his wife Nina, now blind and a small Spokane band relocated onto the banks along Latah Creek in Hangman Valley, just outside the town of Spokane. They lodged beneath what is now Sunset Highway bridge where young boys found it great sport to hurl rocks at their teepees. If Garry went into town, it was said that he gave the white citizens a cold stare. They subsisted on berries, camas root and salmon.

Garry moved from there to Indian Canyon, where a kindly landowner, a Mr. Gavin C Mouat, allowed him to make camp on his land near Indian Canyon. Garry and his blind wife Nina, his daughter, Nellie, and his nephews, Thomas and Titus resided there. Garry was a good husband and had to lift his wife on and off her horse; he then walked the horse slowly with Nina securely strapped on, to his destination. According to friends, Garry was very kind and loving to his family. He moved to Peaceful Valley and Indian Canyon, but he was driven out again.

Garry's life as he had known it was over. He was reduced to that of a pauper and had to butcher cattle to feed his family. Garry's horses were stolen from him by itinerant miners trespassing on Indian lands and professional horse thieves. Gary had no income unless he sold a horse and then only got around $15.00 for it. Garry's daughter, Nellie was a hard worker and earned money for the family by washing clothes for settlers. Garry was supposed to receive $100.00 per year from the Treaty of 1887. He patiently waited for five years and never received a dime. Garry tried to regain possession of his property in Pleasant Valley peacefully using only legal means in court, while his property value soared to $25,000. Garry wrote four books in his lifetime.

Chief Spokane Garry, a great statesman, had devoted his whole life to peace and serving others and had acted as spokesman and interpreter between his people and the Army. Garry had been a friend to the white people and spent countless hours working to save the Spokane people and their lands. He had served as an Anglican evangelist trying to help civilize the people to be Christians. He always was a peace chief, always peaceable and never fought in the Indian Wars. Garry acted as liaison between the white man and the Indians, but was treated like any other Indian.

Garry's once fruitful life had ended in sorrow. His biggest mistake was to trust the palefaces. His industrious life had turned to naught. His luck had turned to tragedy; the white man had scattered his tribe. It was a disastrous ending for a dedicated servant of the people and the downfall of a great man. Half of Garry's tribe had died of smallpox. Spokane's lands were stripped from them. Hundreds of their horses were slaughtered. Millions of buffalo were needlessly killed, the beaver gone. The Spokane way of life was no more. He suffered for siding with the white man. His life became ruin, but he never forgot his God and faith. You could not deny Garry's service to God and his tribe, not to mention 30 years interpreting for the Army and the Bureau of Indian Affairs.

Garry's friends fell away. Some people spoke badly of Garry. Others spoke of him in a better light. A citizen of Spokane said, "I knew him when I was only a boy as he was quite fond of my parents and often stopped at our house for a visit or a smoke with dad," wrote early settler S.T. Woodard. "For years he farmed and raised grain, fruit, and vegetables which he sold (and often gave) to his white neighbors. Dad bought seed potatoes of him and a cow in 1884." (Woodard)

Garry aged, old and feeble; his hair turned from gray to white. He was a broken man and his character was in decline. The last eleven weeks of his life, Garry fell ill and was bedridden.

Garry near the Spokane River Gorge,
the North Bank across river
Public Domain

Mr. Mouat summoned Dr. Harvey, who was at his side when he died at Indian Canyon. Garry passed on January 14, 1892, just eighty one years of age. He had his Bibles, a few Cayuse ponies and teepee. Garry's funeral was conducted on January 16, 1892 by Rev. Mundy of the First Presbyterian Church of Spokane. His family mourned his passing. He was buried in the Greenwood Cemetery in a pauper's grave. Homeless and penniless, his funeral paid by the Spokane County pauper fund. Shortly before Garry's death, a final judgment was made; His property passed into the hands of the white squatter, Schyler D. Doak, an unfair judgment.

Garry became schooled, an excellent student. He was the most educated Indian in the Northwest and spoke three languages. Garry became an evangelist. White missionaries discouraged him and he fell from grace having lived as a civilized Indian. Garry removed his white man's clothes and donned his Indian garb. His life spanned the fur trade era, the coming of white settlers, missionaries, and the U.S. Army. His command of the English language allowed Garry to become a spokesperson, interpreter, and mediator between the Army and his tribe. He was peace chief, peacemaker, and statesman, friend to the white man and Christian evangelist to the Indians, devoted to his people and his God. The Spokane embodied everything that the U.S. Army was against. The Army had killed the Indians in battle, slept with their women, subjected them to diseases, killed off millions of their buffalo (their main food source), took their land, shot their horses, and put them on reservations. Garry never went on the reservation, but lived his life free and uncommitted. His spirit soars!

Nina was later interred beside him. His grave is not far from his place of birth in his homeland. It is a sad ending for a man, who gave so much of himself for others. Garry was 81 years old. He had become a legend in his time and a very wise old chief. Chief Spokan Garry would be remembered for his good deeds.

Last Home Site of
Chief Spokane Garry
Public Domain

Nina at Garry's Gravesite
Public Domain

Chief Spokan Garry's Tombstone
Public Domain

Wood Carving of Chief Garry
Public Domain

Chief Spokane Garry
Historical Marker
Public Domain

# CHAPTER TWELVE
## CHIEF GARRY PARK

Chief Garry was significant to the Spokane tribe, but also to the surrounding tribes and the white man community. He had died in 1892 and passed on a wonderful legacy. A monument to the life of Chief Spokane Garry was erected and dedicated in a special ceremony in August 2011. The celebration was held at Chief Garry Park in Spokane, Washington. His monument had deteriorated over time and was vandalized. It became necessary to erect a new monument in its place with a dedication. It was named, "The Gathering Place." It features details about Chief Spokane Garry, the Spokane tribe and pictures on every aspect of the monument. "The Children of the Sun" is represented by a large steel circle entryway. The copper color of the sun represents the copper that the Spokane people use to make jewelry. A description of aspects of the monument is on a plaque there.

Two hundred were in attendance at the gala ceremony in the Chief Garry Park in north Spokane, Washington. Favored guests were descendents of Chief Garry. Sue Garry and her sister Teresa Iyall Williams were both Tribal Members of the Coeur d'Alene Indian Tribe. Other special guests were Spokane Mayor Verner, four members of the Spokane City Council and many friends of the Spokane Tribe.

Spokane Tribal Members Francis Carlson and Pat Moses arrived with the drum and singers to assist in the celebration of the new monument. They sang traditional songs passed down through generations of Spokane in Garry Park during the dedication.

Tribal Chairman, Greg Abrahamson spoke "It is a day for a great event. Chief Garry was significant not only for the tribe, but to the region, the first tribal leader to learn language-English." Abrahamson welcomed everyone to the ceremony dedication, thanking volunteers who contributed to the project.

Chief Garry Park Spokane, Washington
Courtesy of the Chief Garry Park Neighborhood Council

Dedication Ceremony at Garry Park
Photo Courtesy of the Spokane Tribe of Indians

Abrahamson joined Vice-Chairman Mike Spencer and Council Member Dave Wynecoop to conduct the dedication. The Spokane Tribal Councilmen extended their thanks to all of the volunteers and also the Spokane Union Shops who donated their time and labor to help create the magnificent monument.

A group of Native Americans sang a chorus near the monument. There was a sizeable crowd. The Spokane formed a sun circle. The memorial was held to dedicate a monument to replace a statue of Spokane Garry, destroyed over time by vandals.

Two of Garry's direct descendents spoke. The third sister sent a written message. Other relatives including a great grand-daughter attended, and the Coeur d'Alene tribe took part in the ceremony. Garry's sister, Jeanne Givens, spoke: "I think commemorating Garry is very important. He was the region's first educator. He continually fought for his Upper Spokane and Middle Spokane people to have a permanent homeland. Garry was a Christian and baptized many of his own people. As an interpreter during treaty negotiations, his language skills helped amplify the voice of tribal leaders of their concerns and frustrations, and strengthened their positions for what was fair to their people."

Teresa Ayall-Williams told more of the family lineage: "I am the grand-daughter of Ignus Garry who knew Spokane Garry as a young boy. He lived with him in his teepee. I tell you this because of the great pride we have today to represent Chief Garry. Spokane Garry was first and foremost a teacher," She continued, then told of subsequent generations. "Ayall-Williams is the principal of an elementary school. Her daughter, Nikki Santos, works in higher education with tribal colleges across the country. Givens is a retired teacher, as well as the first Native American woman to hold the office of State Representative in Idaho. How very fitting this place is called 'the Gathering Place.' It brings honor to a place that recognizes Chief Spokane Garry."

Garry Park Fountain
Courtesy of the Chief Garry Park Neighborhood Council

Mildred Parr Ayall, a great-great niece of Spokane Garry, was the longest serving teacher in Washington State. Joseph Garry, a great grandson of Garry was the first Native American U.S. senator from Idaho. "These kinds of miracles just don't happen by happenstance, deep in our family," Ayall said. "It can teach us the strength of family values. It runs in the family."

The Spokane Tribal Council expressed gratitude to Jamie Sijohn, Spokane Tribal Public Relations Director for her part in completion, and other guest speakers were also thanked for leading the fundraising efforts, and overseeing the construction project. Jamie Sijohn brought materials to build the "Gathering Place." She expressed her thanks to all of the school districts and students, who helped raise money for the Garry Fund by collecting coins and donated them to the Heritage Day Celebration the previous year.

Jamie Sijohn introduced 10 year old Victoria Schauer, who made the first donation to the Garry Fund. Victoria solicited funds she had been saving since the age of eight and had raised nearly $30,000 to donate. The committee expressed their gratitude with the gift of a Pendleton blanket. It was amazing how the young people in Spokane went to bat for the park in this drive.

The origin of the design of the Garry Monument was described by Mike Spencer, who was the Spokane Tribal Council vice chairman. The concept had come from a meeting at Wellpinits High School. Elders, parents, and teachers had joined a group of a dozen freshman students having difficulty transitioning to high school. A traditional drum was struck while the classroom provided the beat, as ancestral songs were sung. The students were given words of encouragement. They were reminded of Chief Spokan Garry and how he received his education away from home. Garry's education and a circular shape led to the design of the monument. Its base was a flagstone entry, circles of the drum, salmon, and the sun circle all relate to the tribe.

Statuary with Garry Photo
Photo Courtesy of the Spokane Tribe of Indians

Funds to erect the monument were donated. Chief Garry left a legacy in Spokane as a leader, peacemaker and educator. His life affected by others. He was driven down by his age, and sadly tossed aside.

Chief Spokane Garry was not forgotten, because in 1925, the Spokane Chapter of the Daughters of the American Revolution raised a huge monument of granite over Garry's grave. In 1932 a Spokane City Park was dedicated to him and named Chief Garry Park. A school in Spokane was named Garry Middle School.

In 1979, a wonderful statue of Garry was erected in Chief Garry Park. The statue in the elements began to crumble and vandals broke off the fingers. Because of the damage, it was ordered by the city to be removed from the park in 2008 and was reduced to a mere pile of rubble.

The City of Spokane announced that they were planning to replace the Garry statue with an abstract "totem" sculpture. Instead, a grass roots group drive raised $40,000 for a circular stone monument to be dedicated at the park, complete with an ancient pictograph, steel Salmon, and interpretive signs portraying Garry's life. Chief Spokan Garry's eyes again survey his homeland.

Special thanks to the schools for their coin drives: Wellpinit School District, Roosevelt and Seth Woodard Elementary Schools, and Northwest Christian School District for their fundraising efforts.

On the northwest corner of Chief Garry Park lies the monument in north Spokane, Washington. To help maintain the monument, donations are being accepted. If a person would be interested in donating, mail your donation to Chief Garry Fund, Attention   Jamie Si john, P.O. Box 100, Wellpinit, Washington, 99040.

Abstract Totem features circular stone monument with ancient
pictograph, steel Salmon, and signs portraying Garry's life.
Photo Courtesy of the Spokane Indian Tribe

Spokane Garry's Daughter Nellie
Public Domain

Grand Daughter Alice Garry
Public Domain

Yakima Woman
Public Domain

140

Spokane Jim Elijah 1920
Public Domain

Spokane Brave, Bird Rattle in Full Garb 1910
Public Domain

Dugout Canoes Spokane Indian Method of Transportation
Public Domain

Spokane Indian Princess in Full Regalia
Public Domain

Spokane Powwow Dancer
Photo Courtesy of Wikipedia.org

Pend d' Oreille (Rings in Ears) Warrior or Chief
Public Dominion

Spokane Indian Papoose 1899
Photo Courtesy of Wikipedia.org

Spokane Indian Encampment
Public Domain

Spokane Wickiup
Public Domain

Spokane Indians in Parade 1900's
Downtown Spokane Washington
Public Domain

Sign at Reservation Entrance
Photo Courtesy of Wikipedia.org

Children at Fort Spokane Indian School
Photo Courtesy of Wikipedia.org

Spokane Indians at Fort Spokane 1883
Public Domain

Spokane Father Teaches Son Archery
Photo Courtesy of Wikipedia.org

Walla Walla Mother and Child
Photo Courtesy of Wikipedia.org

Spokane Tribe in 1800's
Public Domain

Colville Indian Family
Photo Courtesy of Wikipedia.org

Nez Perce Woman, 1903.
Public Domain

Salmon
Photo Courtesy of Wikipedia.org

Chief Joseph of the Nez Perce Nation
Photo Courtesy of Wikipedia.org

Spokane's Lizzie Hammer Quintana and Grandma on Horseback
Public Domain

Spokane Indians on Reservation
Public Domain

Spokans by Spokane River
Public Domain

Kalispells, Salish, Skitswish, and Spokans at the Spokane Fair
Public Domain

Indian Fishing at Kettle Falls
Public Domain

Native American on Washington Reservation
Photo Courtesy of Wikipedia.org

1800's Plateau Maiden
Photo Courtesy of
Wikipedia.org

Coastal and Plateau Indians
Photo Courtesy of
Wikipedia.org

# Index

171

# Bibliography

Jesset, Thomas E., *Chief Spokan Garry* 1811-1892, Brings Press, Minneapolis, 1960

Lewis, William S., *The Case of Spokane Garry*, Ye Galleon Press, Fairfield, Washington. 1987.

Salish-Pend d' Oreille Culture Committee and Elders Cultural Advisory Council Confederated Salish and Kootenai Tribes, *The Salish People and the Lewis and Clark Expedition*, University of Nebraska Press, Lincoln, 2008.

# End Notes

End Note: Garry's treaty speeches: pg. 83-107 "Chief Spokan Garry," Thomas E. Jesset

# Citing Electronic
## Publications

<http//www. athena.ecs.csus.edu/~ buckley/CSc21/Chief Spokane Garry.pdf>

<http://www. crossroadsarchive.org/spokan-garry>

<http://discoveryrobots.org/spokanehistory/spogarry.html>

<https://www.en.wikipedia.org/wiki/Chief_Garry>

<http://www.en.wikipedia.org/wiki/TshimakainMission>

<http://www.fws.gov/species/species_accounts/bio_salm.html>

<http://www.historylink.org/File/8713>

<http//www.historylink.org/index.cfm?DisplayPage=output.c fm&file_id=8713>

<http://www.spokanetribe.com/about>

<http://www.u-s-story.com/pages/h1570.html>

<http://www.washingtonhistory.org/files/library/Garry-biography.pdf>

<http://www.washingtonhistory.org/files/library/Garry-biography>

## Amazon Kindle

Jackson, Dave and Neta, *Exiled to the Red River*, Bethany House Publishers, Grand Rapids, Michigan, 2003.

McMurray, Douglas, *The Forgotten Awakening*, Deep River Publishing, Sisters, Oregon, 2011.

## Magazines

Real West Magazine, February 1974 Edition, Spokan Garry, Amazing Indian Chief, Derby, Wisconsin.

Photo by David
Brooks

**Author explores inside of a 19th century
stone house in southeastern Oregon.**
### About the Author

Born in Lexington, Nebraska, Author Robert Bolen, B.A. has a degree in Archeology/Anthropology. In an Archeology class, he was informed that because of his Mongolian eye-fold, he was part Indian. In 1755, a Bolen ancestor was taken captive by Delaware Indians and later rescued with her baby daughter, Robb's Great, Great, Grandmother. When rescued, the poor girl (just 17) was scalped, but she lived. A French scalp was the size of a silver dollar. Family says she combed her hair to hide the scar and lived to be well over one hundred years of age. Bolen's served under George Washington in the American Revolution. In 1777, the author's ancestors erected Fort Bolin, near Cross Creek, Pennsylvania for protection from Indian attacks. Two ancestors were killed in Kentucky by Shawnee Indians allied to the British. Great Granddad Gilbert Bolen rode with the Ohio Fourth Cavalry in the Civil War under General Sherman. In 1866, Gilbert brought his wife and six children west to Nebraska in a Conestoga wagon. Gran-dad Denver Colorado Bolen knew Buffalo Bill Cody in western Nebraska. Bolen is an authority on Indian artifacts and glass trade beads. Robb and Dori Bolen reside in Nampa, Idaho, near Boise. Robb owns the website, Fort Boise Bead Trader.com.

175

# More Books
# by Robert D. Bolen

**Smoke Signals & Wagon Tracks**
**American Indian Tribes of Idaho**
**Blackfeet Raiders,**
**Nomads of the North**
**The Horse Indians**
**The Lakota Sioux Indians**
**The Medicine Crow Indians**
**"The Snake People,"**
**The Northern Shoshoni Indians**
**War Chief Paulina & His Renegade**
**Band of Paiutes**
**War Chief Joseph and the Indian Wars**
**The Paiute Indian Nation**

# DRUM and HOOFBEATS

by Robert D. Bolen

THE LATEST BOOK WRITTEN
BY ROBERT D. BOLEN
## DRUM & HOOFBEATS

# PHOTOGRAPHS
# COURTESY OF
# AZUSA Publishing, LLC
## 3575 S. Fox Street
## Englewood, CO 80110

Email: azusa@azusapublishing.com

Phone Toll-free: 888-783-0077

Phone/Fax: 303-783-0073

**Graphic Design Services**

**Provided by**

# DESIGNER

Cover Design

Book Layout

Text and Page Formatting

Editing

Photo Clarification and Enhancement

Etc.

Bonnie Fitzpatrick

208.249.2635

bjfitz 777@msn.com